C000071044

War Since 1990

War Since 1990

Jeremy Black

THE
SOCIAL
AFFAIRS
UNIT

© The Social Affairs Unit 2009
All rights reserved

British Library Cataloguing in Publication Data
A catalogue record of this book is available from the British Library

All views expressed in this publication are those of the author, not those
of the Social Affairs Unit, its Trustees, Advisers or Director

Printed and bound in the United Kingdom

ISBN-13: 978-1-904863-36-6

Social Affairs Unit
314–322 Regent Street
London W1B 5SA
www.socialaffairsunit.org.uk

The Social Affairs Unit has no responsibility for the persistence or
accuracy of URLs for websites referred to in this publication, and does
not guarantee that any content on such websites is, or will remain,
accurate or appropriate.

For
Julian Lewis

CONTENTS

ABOUT THE AUTHOR

Jeremy Black is Professor of History at the University of Exeter. Graduating from Cambridge with a Starred First, he did postgraduate work at Oxford and then taught at Durham, eventually as Professor, before moving to Exeter in 1996. He has lectured extensively in Australia, Canada, Denmark, France, Germany, Ireland, Italy, Japan, the Netherlands, New Zealand, Norway, Singapore, Slovenia, Spain and the USA, where he has held visiting chairs at West Point, Texas Christian University and Stillman College. A past council member of the Royal Historical Society, Black is a Fellow of the Royal Society for the Encouragement of Arts, Manufactures and Commerce, a Senior Fellow of the Foreign Policy Research Institute and a trustee of Agora. He was appointed to the Order of Membership of the British Empire for services to stamp design. In 2008, he received the Samuel Eliot Morison Prize of the Society for Military History.

He is, or has been, on a number of editorial boards, including the *Journal of Military History,* the journal of the Royal United Services Institute, *Media History* and *History Today,* and was Editor of *Archives.*

His books include *War and the World, 1450–2000* (Yale), *The British Seaborne Empire* (Yale), *Maps and History* (Yale) and *European Warfare in a Global Context, 1600–1815* (Routledge).

PREFACE

Historians are not supposed to write on the present, let alone the future. Within the profession, such writing is regarded sniffily at best and, more commonly, with the criticism, indeed opprobrium, directed at those who are supposed to have abandoned mission, or, at least, the craft of the trade. If history is an attempt to employ sources, especially archival sources, in order to understand the past, and if, for many scholars, there is an aspiration to produce definitive accounts of the past, then this book is a flagrant breach of the conventions of history.

It is certainly the case that it is difficult to gain historical perspectives on current events. The public view tends to be less harsh, but there is still a supposition that historians should tackle the past, not the present, let alone the future. Moreover, the policy implications of the historical analysis and judgement of very recent times are immediate and likely to be hotly contested, even if that analysis is expressed only in terms of what is emphasised in the narrative. In other words, the politics of historical interpretation – always an issue, but usually a fairly muted one in the study of the distant past – is unavoidable in discussion of contemporary affairs. The importance of warfare in modern politics further highlights this problem.

So an explanation is required. First, I see history not only as an engagement with the past but also as a habit of mind that, while indeed based on the study of the past, can also be applied to present and future. I would describe this habit of mind as a questioning one, sceptical of received truths and, therefore, anti-authoritarian. Indeed, I would take this argument further and argue that historians should try to study the present and consider the future, not only in order to acquire perspectives that could be usefully employed in their consideration of the past but also because this use of their skill is a valuable public good. If historians do not do so, others will apply the past with probably less understanding and skill, a point amply demonstrated in my *The Curse of History* (2008).

Second, although I am no postmodernist, I doubt that we can produce definitive accounts of the past, however valuable they might be in theory, while I think that quasi-definitive assessments are perforce on matters of very narrow span. Thus, I am dubious about the validity and extent of the qualitative differences so readily claimed on behalf of historical work on the past as opposed to the discussion of the present.

Third, I note that, whereas British academic historians generally fight shy of an engagement with the present, this reluctance is not true of their counterparts in many other countries. This situation seriously calls into question the assumptions, if not ideology, that dominate and define the power structures of the British historical profession. This ideology would repay separate study.

As far as *War Since 1990* is concerned, there seems particularly strong reasons why I should engage with present and future conflict. First, such conflict is, and will be, important and will help define the world of succeeding generations. Indeed, the extent to which war can do so is a revenge of the particular and the moment against the teleological certainties of models of long-term historical development. Possibly as a result, many historians who do not specialise in military history are reluctant to pay it sufficient attention.

Second, alongside detailed studies of aspects of eighteenth-century warfare, much of my work on military history has deployed a series of related conceptual arguments that are also important for the current situation and, indeed, for the future. In particular, I have argued for the need to emphasise, for any particular period, the variety of military circumstances and developments as well as the extent to which the understanding of force and the definitions of victory and defeat are guided primarily by cultural assumptions. This view has led me to be wary about interpretations of military capability and change based on material culture and, more particularly, technological superiority. Linked to this, I emphasise the need to see tasks or goals rather than capabilities as the central context for, and motor of, change in war-making.

I have also argued the need to consider non-Western developments, not in terms of some failure to adopt and adapt Western methods and paradigms but rather as a response to specific circumstances and cultures.[1] The understanding of non-Western developments is crucial if the potential of Western war-making is to be assessed accurately, an assessment that has not always been apparent in recent years. Indeed, it is particularly pertinent to consider these arguments in light of conflict since 1990, and this is a major theme of this book.

Third, as a related point, there is considerable confusion as to the definition and application of the concept of modern war, and this book is intended to contribute to discussion of the issue. In particular, there is confusion about the relationship between modern and total war and, indeed, about the definition and historical location of the latter.[2] In practice, total war is, and was, not necessarily modern, and modern war is not necessarily total. This point is a crucial critique of the teleological commonplace of the standard narrative and analysis of long-term military developments.

In thinking about the topic, I benefited greatly from the opportunity to attend the 2008 conference of the Society for Military History and would like to thank the Society for inviting me to give the opening plenary lecture and for awarding me the Samuel Eliot Morison prize. I have also benefited from the opportunity to speak at the 2008 Asia-Pacific Conference for Senior Military Officers, at the 2008 West Point Summer Seminar in Military History, at the Singapore Staff College, and at Adelphi University, Texas A&M University and the University of North Texas. I would also like to thank Kevin Farrell, Frank Hamilton, Paul Herbert, Rob Johnson, Tony Kelly and Rana Mitter for commenting on an earlier draft. Their generosity in doing so is much appreciated. None is responsible for any of the errors that remain. As ever, Michael Mosbacher has proved a most supportive publisher, and I would like to thank Liz O'Donnell for her editorial skills.

It is a great pleasure that Julian Lewis has accepted the dedication of this book. Aside from being a parliamentarian of note and a leading specialist on British defence issues, Julian is also the author of one of the most thoughtful historical studies on British defence planning.[3] That he is a kind host and an agreeable companion is also worthy of note. Julian and I also share the conviction that defence planning and procurement need to be based not on the threat of the moment, important as that will be, but on considerations of long-term security considerations that require an understanding of past, present and future. Part of the pleasure of writing this book was considering what Julian would make of it.

CHAPTER 1

INTRODUCTION:
BRINGING TOGETHER TWO NARRATIVES

The present dominates the past because we see the latter through the prism of today. For Western commentators, everything summed up by the word 'Iraq' is apt to be particularly imposing. This situation has been the case since 2003, although readings of the war and its aftermath have varied considerably. As Saddam Hussein's unprovoked invasion of Kuwait in 1990 was directly responsible for the Gulf War of 1990–1, the major conventional conflict of that decade, Iraq has played a key role in analysis from the outset of the period covered in this book. It is safe to predict that this will continue to be the case, and especially so in the anglophone literature.

Yet, as I seek to show in this book, this focus is not only understandable but also very misleading, because these conflicts did not launch new developments. Instead, they represented tendencies and, in particular, methods of warfighting, which were already present. Moreover, these wars can detract from the other conflicts of the period, conflicts to which I try to devote due attention in so far as the space permits. It is instructive, for example, when lecturing on this period, to ask which war has led to the most casualties and to be repeatedly told, in both Britain and the USA, 'Iraq', meaning the 2003 struggle, when, in practice, casualty figures in both Zaire/Congo and Sudan have been considerably higher.

This contrast is part of a pattern of underplaying non-Western conflict. Try asking, 'Which war in the period 1946–80 had the most combatants or highest casualties?' The answer usually given is 'Vietnam', meaning the Vietnam conflict when the Americans were involved (and not, more accurately, the longer pattern of post-1945 conflict in that country); the correct reply would be the Chinese Civil War of 1946–9. Or again, asking about the 1980s and being told, notably, but not only, in Britain, the Anglo-Argentinean Falklands War (1982) and not that between Iran and Iraq (1980–8). The latter is a conflict that repays examination, not least because it helped condition attitudes to war in both Iran and Iraq and also led Saddam Hussein to invade Kuwait in 1990 in order to try to recoup his costs.

This point about relative attention leads towards the central conceptual argument of the book. By focusing on the Western narrative of military history, and, especially, on the themes of technological proficiency as deployed in conventional warfare, analysts, both historians and, more seriously, those working on the present, have tended to underplay the non-West. Or rather, the latter has been considered largely in terms of the adoption of Western weaponry and methods. This approach, however, is less than a complete account. In particular, it offers a misleading narrative for non-Western warfare, one characterised by a lack of due attention and an absence of understanding. Indeed, there is a tendency to simplify non-Western military circumstances, and goals and forms of warfare, and this tendency can even be seen in some of the literature that argues for the need to reconsider the future of conflict.

The failure to understand non-Western warfare, moreover, is significant, not simply because we ought to try to understand the situation around the world but also because the effectiveness of Western forces requires such an understanding, as sometimes, more bluntly, does the survival of Western expeditionary units. Thus, those who are concerned about Western military effectiveness need to support an approach to military environments and conflict as they are, and not as might be wished, whether militarily, politically or both, and whether describing the present or the future. In backing such an approach, the commentators risk accusations of relativism and defeatism, but that is misleading. It is in order to avoid defeat that one notes weaknesses, not in order to welcome it. Ignoring such weaknesses is a sign not of heroism and bravery but, rather, of folly. Ignorance will not be the basis for a triumph of the will.

In short, this book is a contribution to military education, by which I mean education about the military as much as education for the military. Indeed, the former is more necessary, because there is a widespread public ignorance about military issues and problems, an ignorance that is also apparent in political circles and seems to have been especially characteristic of the policy-making of the Labour governments in Britain since 1997. This ignorance may owe something to a lack of military experience but, more generally, reflects the emphasis on domestic issues and social policy in political concern. This emphasis is an aspect of the expeditionary warfare mindset, for war somehow seems separate and detachable from more urgent domestic concerns. This situation is a recipe for poor military morale and for failures in policy-making.

The period since 1990 has seen a particularly abrupt shift in the discussion of Western military proficiency. In the 1990s, alongside the misleading claim that nuclear weaponry and, subsequently, the end of the Cold War had made war obsolete,[1] there was a triumphalist focus on high-spectrum capability, a focus that continued the Cold War emphasis on such weaponry and related doctrine, especially on the part of the USA. In the 1990s, this focus was linked to an assertion that, in the shape of a supposed Revolution in Military Affairs (see Chapter 2), this capability had changed – indeed transformed – the nature of current and future warfare and that understanding this change, and transforming the military accordingly, would ensure victory. This thesis received powerful support from the role in particular of air power in the defeat of Iraq in 1991 and of Serbia in 1995 and 1999, and in the rapid overthrow of the Taliban in Afghanistan in 2001. The thesis appeared to reach a new level of validity with the rapid overthrow of Saddam Hussein in 2003, as the Iraqi military was speedily routed, and by an American-led coalition force significantly smaller (and even more focused on American strength) than that deployed against Iraq in 1991.

The aftermath of the 2003 invasion, however, suggested that much of this triumphalist discussion had been misplaced. This reconceptualisation was not a case of revisionism, in that the Iraqi military had indeed been totally routed and the regime completely overthrown. Moreover, the insurgency did not prove the basis of a Baathist revanche. However, alongside this triumphalist narrative, and greatly compromising the conclusions drawn from it, there was a different narrative that became increasingly prominent in Iraq, one of the limitations of conventional forces and of the notion of a clear hierarchy of military success and, instead, of the variety of means of effective conflict. The term 'effectiveness' has to be employed with care, as the insurgents and terrorists in Iraq were scarcely creative politically or socially, but they were able to challenge the verdict of the invasion, and, indeed, the confidence that the leading military power, the USA, could employ force to secure its purposes.

If this situation suggested the vitality of non-Western military practices, and the challenges they posed, this point was underlined in 2006 by the difficulties the Israeli military experienced at the hands of Hizbullah in southern Lebanon and, also in 2006, by the resurgence of the Taliban in Afghanistan. In each case, it is possible to debate the extent to which the Western force was actually defeated, and there is a need not to assume a greater degree of success for insurrections than is merited. This is a point more generally true of the post-1945 world, with its romanticism of left-wing guerrillas and, more seriously, the failure to note the military and political limitations of such warfare. Nevertheless, there is no doubt that each of the above episodes represented a major blow to the use of military means to secure a political response, not least that of creating an impression of success. From that perspective, the Israelis were unsuccessful, contributing to serious political problems in Lebanon and, indeed, Israel, while in Afghanistan the impression was created of a situation slipping out of control.

In each case, as earlier with the North Vietnamese/Viet Cong, the political prospectus of the non-Western force was vicious, deadly and dangerous, but that provides even more of a reason why their military narrative has to be included. To present modern warfare in terms of a comforting account of Western proficiency, as was particularly the case in the 1990s and the early 2000s (and possibly in conscious reaction to the pessimistic post-Vietnam situation in the 1970s), will not make us any safer, nor will it help ensure the effective planning and training that is necessary. The conviction that modern, limited warfare could be defined and, then, fine-tuned to achieve victory and suit Western political purposes, not least in terms of liberal interventionism, proved particularly feckless. Instead, the defence of Western values requires an understanding of our fragility and of the flawed nature of the standard account. Analysis informed by historical insights can contribute greatly to this goal, and this book seeks to clarify a number of troubling themes for the Western powers.

CHAPTER 2

A CONVENTIONAL ACCOUNT, 1990–2000

Modern technology and total power were key themes in the understanding of twentieth-century Western warfare. If their deadliest manifestation was the American use of two atomic bombs against Japan in August 1945 in order to bring the Second World War to a close, this was only because the far more extensive, powerful and varied nuclear arsenals subsequently built up by the major powers were not used. This theme of the competition of potent and technologically advanced systems, however, appeared less pertinent in the late 1980s as the Cold War eased, ebbed and ended. The advent of Mikhail Gorbachev as Soviet leader in 1985 was followed by nuclear limitation agreements with the USA, by Soviet disengagement, especially, in 1988, from Afghanistan and by the end of Soviet-sponsored Cuban expeditionary operations in Africa.

The collapse of European Communism and the Soviet Union in 1989–91 took this process unexpectedly forward but also created what was at once a new military landscape and the need and opportunity for new military doctrines. In the USA, the discussion was largely in terms of the Revolution in Military Affairs (RMA). More widely cited than defined, and meaning too many things to too many people, the RMA in fact had a number of meanings and associations,[1] which, in combination, suggested not only its usefulness to its advocates but also its misleading character. Indeed, the RMA was symptomatic of a set of cultural and political assumptions that tell us more about the aspirations of the 1990s than they do about any objective assessment of military capabilities. In particular, the RMA reflected the desire for unquestioned potency without any matching need to accept conscription, a war economy, or many casualties, and, in part, can therefore be seen as a response to the decline of the warrior ethos.[2]

The RMA also reflected the assertion of Western, more particularly American, superiority, as well as the ideology of mechanisation that had long been important to American military thought. This ideology was crucial, for capability, if not worth, was defined in a machine age in terms of machines, which were then used to assert and demonstrate superiority. This approach also appeared to provide a ready measure of assessing the strength of different states and, indeed, civilisations. Strength could not only be assessed, let alone measured. It was also apparently possible to shape the changing equations of strength by investing in new capability at the cutting edge of technological progress.

Thus, the RMA was an expression of the modern secular technological belief system that is prevalent in the West and easily meshes with theories of modernisation that rest on the adoption of new technology and related concepts. Moreover, it was particularly crucial to Americans that the RMA was an American-led military revolution as it apparently underlined American proficiency and also offered a way to look at the world in which this proficiency appeared to be without end, or, at least, would be redefined in terms that the Americans were confident they could determine. In accordance with a long-term tendency in American military (and political) thinking,[3] the RMA met the American need to believe in the possibility of high-intensity conflict and of total victory, with opponents shocked and awed into accepting defeat, rather than offering the ambiguous and qualified nature of modern victory. In addition, the certainty of the RMA appeared to offer a defence against the threats posed by the spread of earlier technologies, such as long-range missiles and atomic warheads, as well as of new ones, such as bacteriological warfare, and of whatever might follow. Providing invulnerability, the RMA seemed to keep the Americans ahead.

This point was taken on board by politicians who understood the need to offer security. Standing for president, George W. Bush, in September 1999, told an audience at the Citadel, a prominent military academy, that 'the best way to keep the peace is to redefine war on our terms.' Once elected, he declared at the Citadel in 2001, 'The first priority is to speed the transformation of our military.' Indeed, the sense that already established military structures and systems were part of the problem, and not a key means to the solution, helped explain the very poor relations between Donald Rumsfeld, Bush's unfortunate choice as Secretary of Defense from 2001 to 2006, and many of America's senior commanders.

This tension was related to the totalising culture and prospectus offered by the RMA and the transformation of the military that was its institutional and doctrinal expression. The belief in clear problem and obvious solution proved potent, especially in a political and institutional culture that did not welcome ambiguity or doubt. Ironically, many of those today who advocate counter-insurgency (COIN) doctrine as the ultimate solution to everything said the same, earlier, and in a misleading fashion, about the RMA and Transformation.

Transformation entailed a move from large 'platform-centric' formations and units, such as armoured divisions, to groupings which were orientated on particular missions and which were designed to act in a more agile fashion. These groupings grew on, and were located in, a matrix of networks of sensors, information processors and shooters. Thus, 'network-centric' warfare was the goal as it was believed to take military capability to a new plane of effectiveness.

Rumsfeld felt that the Pentagon was overly bureaucratic and that it had failed to adapt to the post-Cold War world and to the military needs and opportunities this produced. Rumsfeld created the Office of Force Transformation, appointing a retired vice admiral, Arthur Cebrowksi, as its Director. Cebrowski was very commited to the idea of network-centric warfare and its role in capability enhancement.[4] Rumsfeld responded to such ideas by using them as an opportunity to challenge the established Pentagon processes and current American commitments. In particular, Rumsfeld felt that the military should focus on war-winning, not such peacekeeping as the Kosovo mission, and that the route to the former was a smaller and more adaptable military. Thus, the failure to send sufficient troops to Iraq was of a piece with Rumsfeld's intentions.

The RMA can be located very much in terms of a particular moment in American strategic thought and military politics, one of boldness of conception about America's ability to act as a force for good, a boldness held in liberal as much as neo-conservative circles.[5] Indeed, those who touted the RMA and the quest to achieve it helped to get the USA into its current military predicament. At the same time, the ideas summarised as the RMA could serve to support a range of Western political strategies, including those of both isolationalists and interventionists. In practice, the RMA particularly lent itself to the cause of American unilateralism, and this was most clearly espoused by neo-conservatives, although unilateralism was more generally a characteristic of American attitudes, and the neo-conservative use of it drew on a long tradition. The combination of unilateralism and the RMA can then be assessed in the context of the *relative* American decline in a more multi-centred world, a process that began in the 1960s with the rise in the Japanese and German economies, and which has gathered pace over the past decade with those of China and India.[6]

At the same time, it is important to be cautious about suggesting too much coherence and consistency in the idea of an RMA, a point which is underlined by consideration of military revolutions which are supposed to have occurred earlier. A less harsh view than that just summarised can be advanced if the RMA is presented, instead, as a doctrine designed to meet political goals and, thus, to shape or encourage technological developments and operational and tactical suppositions accordingly, rather than to allow technological constraints to shape doctrine and, thus, to risk the danger of inhibiting policy.

That is a pertinent conceptual point, but, in reality, much discussion of the RMA, especially, but not only, in the USA, did seem to suggest a technology-driven and defined warfare. A lot of the technology was focused on overcoming the problems of command and control posed by the large number of units operating simultaneously and on fulfilling the opportunities for command and control gained by successfully overcoming this challenge, and thus aggregating sensors, shooters and deciders to achieve a precise mass effect from dispersed units.

Advocates of the RMA progressed to talking about 'space control' and the 'empty battlefield' of the future, where wars would be waged for 'information dominance' – in other words, control of satellites, telecommunications and computer net-works. The American military thus contrasted its information grids and networks, which were to be safeguarded in wartime, with hostile ones which had to be destroyed. Integrated commu-nications technologies were designed to enhance offensive and defensive information warfare capability, while better commu-nications permitted both more integrated fire support and the use of surveillance to allow more accurate targeting. All were to be achieved rapidly in accord with political and military needs, not least, in the latter case, getting within opposing decision cycles. Surveillance capability also enabled commanders to have greater knowledge of the locations of their own units, as with the use of the American Blue Force Tracker system during the invasion of Iraq in 2003.[7]

The new weaponry was indicative of priorities. There was a stress on cheaper, unmanned platforms intended to replace recon-naissance and attack aircraft. Whether termed UAVs (unmanned aerial vehicles) or RPVs (remotely piloted vehicles), these plat-forms were designed to take the advantage of missiles further by providing mobile platforms from which they could be fired or bombs dropped. Platforms do not require on-site crew and, thus, can be used without risk to the life or liberty of personnel, and, as a consequence, they can be low-flying as the risk of losses of pilots to anti-aircraft fire has been removed. These losses, and the problems they posed, not least the prospect of hostage-type situa-tions with the pressures they entailed, contributed to the priorities for a new air power.

In addition, at least in theory, the logistical burden of air power is reduced with unmanned platforms. So also is the cost, as these platforms are less expensive than manned counterparts, and there are big savings in pilot training. Unmanned platforms should also be more compact and 'stealthy' (i.e. less easy to detect), while the acceleration and manoeuvrability of such platforms would no longer be limited by G-forces that would render pilots uncon-scious. These points suggest that the future value of large aircraft carriers is questionable, at least in so far as they carry manned planes. It should be possible, instead, to provide smaller vessels able to launch unmanned platforms.

In 1999, unarmed drones were employed extensively for surveillance over Kosovo in order to send information on bomb damage and refugee columns; and in Afghanistan in 2001 and Iraq in 2003 armed drones were used as firing platforms. The 8-metre (26-foot) American-produced Predator drone, with its operating radius of 805 kilometres (500 miles), flight duration of up to 40 hours, cruising speed of 129 kilometres per hour (80 miles per hour) and normal operating altitudes of 4,572 metres (15,000 feet), was designed to destroy air-defence batteries and command centres. It can be used in areas contaminated by chemical or germ warfare, and its software is programmed to be able to tell if the intended target has moved close to civilians and to suggest a change of plan accordingly. The use of drones rapidly spread, with Israel employing them, while in 2008 the Russian-backed breakaway region of Abkhazia claimed to destroy seven reconnaissance drones sent from Georgia (the Caucasus republic and not the American state). Israel provided Georgia with drones.

The capability of unmanned platforms is enhanced by designing them to work within systems or networks that bring together dispersed units and different types of weapons, and, moreover, from a number of environments: space, air, land and sea. These systems operate on the basis of high and sustained rates of information. By 2000, American military surveillance satellites, with their digital sensors and their almost instantaneous transmission over encrypted radio links, had a resolution better than 100 millimetres (4 inches). The potential of this surveillance became a major international issue in 2002 as the USA claimed that satellite information made it clear that Iraq was stockpiling weapons of mass destruction and evading the ground-search programme being carried out by UN inspectors. This episode apparently highlighted the extent to which it was possible to overcome one of the major characteristics of totalitarian regimes – information management.

America is at the forefront of such technology, although it is not alone in its development goals and, in order to recoup some of the cost, is likely to sell advanced weapons to allies. It is difficult, however, to control the process of technology transfer. For example, in 2000, the Americans threatened action if Israel, which had benefited greatly from such transfer, sold an airborne radar system to China that could be used against America's ally Taiwan.

In any assessment of the technology, it is necessary to note the contrast that is readily apparent between sea or air power and land capability, a difference in perspective that explains a great deal of how the American military ended up in its present position. Superiority in forms of military technology and military-industrial complexes are more important in sea and air environments, where their effect is fundamental; but precisely the same forms of superiority in technology and industry have a far smaller impact so far as land power goes. A general theoretical conclusion that emerges is that factors that help provide a capability advantage, or that cause success (the two are not synonymous), in one context are not necessarily relevant in others. Partly as a result, the RMA as an ideology is in many respects an air-power ideology and one that represents the extension of the latter into space. In noting that, however, it is important not to overlook the extent to which there was also a process of major change in the other services (see pp. 38–40).

Some of the discussion of the RMA, not least the emphasis on network-centre warfare implied, or even assumed, that the world is an isotropic (uniform) surface, made knowable, pliable and controllable by new technology. However, it is necessary to understand not simply the limitations of the latter but also the limitations of a technology-driven account of capability and change. This account entails the misapplication of tactical capabilities and lessons to operational goals and of operational lessons to strategic goals, a misapplication that readily stems from the tendency to take an overly optimistic view of technological capabilities and from the disinclination to appreciate the political dynamics and measures of strategic goals and issues. This view can lead to the illusion that fresh technologies can, and thus will, bring new powers and, therefore, that problems can be readily banished. That is not the appropriate military analysis and tasking for the twenty-first century. Thus, picking apart the RMA is not some parlour game but, instead, is crucial to the assessment of Western capability.

The RMA suggested novelty as the key theme of the 1990s, but, in practice, there was more continuity in war-making, not least because it was Cold War weaponry, training and doctrine which were employed and tested. This use of Cold War assets was recognisably the case with the USA and involved in particular the new grasp of the operational dimension of war, a grasp that had developed in the 1980s as a manoeuvrist doctrine developed to aid planning for a mobile defence of Western Europe in the event of Soviet attack. This doctrine and planning was linked to the post-Vietnam revitalisation of the army, revitalisation that involved a process of transformation or, at least, redirection. Continuity with the Cold War was particularly the case because the major war the USA fought in the 1980s was at the outset of the decade and was waged against a military largely equipped by the Soviet Union. This was the First Gulf War, a conflict set off by the Iraqi invasion of neighbouring Kuwait. A far smaller and weaker target than Iran, which Iraq had unsuccessfully attacked in 1980, oil-rich Kuwait rapidly fell on 2 August 1990. Six days later, Saddam Hussein declared Kuwait to be Iraq's nineteenth province.

The response defined high-spectrum warfare for the decade. Concerned about the impact of Iraqi expansion in the centre of the world's foremost region of oil production and, even more, oil exports, George H. W. Bush, the American President, encouraged by Margaret Thatcher, the British Prime Minister, rapidly began diplomatic and military preparations for conflict. Iraq's failure to press on to attack Saudi Arabia ensured that the initiative thereafter rested with its opponents, although Saudi Arabia was a far more formidable challenge than Kuwait, particularly due to its size, the strength of its armed forces and its close political links with the USA, while the element of surprise had been lost.

On 3 August 1990, two American carrier groups were ordered towards the region, a key display as well as means of support, and, on 8 August, in response to a Saudi request, delivered two days earlier, for ground troops, the first American forces arrived. The build-up of (mostly American) coalition forces in neighbouring Saudi Arabia benefited from the availability of Saudi oil and bases. This build-up was matched by a blockade intended to hit Iraqi trade, particularly exports of oil, Iraq's major resource.

Saddam's refusal to meet a UN deadline for withdrawal from Kuwait led, on 17 January 1991, to the start of a major air offensive on Iraq. Although aircraft from twelve countries were involved, the Americans were central to the offensive, which worked because of the rapid success in overcoming the sophisticated Iraqi anti-aircraft system. Saddam had used French and Soviet technology to produce an integrated system in which computers linked radars and missiles, but the system, although advanced for the day, was overcome. Moreover, Iraq's heavily outnumbered air force did not intervene in strength. Instead, the MiG-29s flew to Iran where they were added to its air force.

The Allied air offensive benefited from state-of-the-art American weaponry: B-2 stealth bombers able to minimise radar detection bombed targets in Baghdad – one of the most heavily defended cities in the world – and did so with impunity, while the Americans made highly effective use of guided bombs. Thermal-imaging laser-designation systems were employed to guide the bombs to their target, and pilots launched bombs into the cone of the laser beam in order to score a direct hit. The destruction of the air-defence system, with only one aircraft lost (to an Iraqi MiG-29) on the first night, was a triumph not only for weaponry but also for planning that made full use of the opportunities presented by the Allied weapons, while also out-thinking the Iraqis – for example by getting them to bring their radars to full power and thus exposing them to Coalition attack.

The use of stealth and precision had important operational and strategic consequences as it meant that it was possible to employ a direct air assault aimed at overcoming the entire Iraqi air system rather than an incremental roll-back campaign. Moreover, the situation on the ground was transformed. As a consequence of the air assault, Iraqi forces were to be short of supplies, their command and control system was heavily disrupted so that they could not 'understand' the battle, and their morale was low. Both at the time and subsequently, RMA advocates were to make much of the potential of air power and to draw considerable attention to the 1991 campaign. Air power was indeed crucial to the first three phases of the operation: destroying Iraqi command and control, isolating the battlefield and weakening Iraqi forces in the Kuwaiti theatre of operations.[8]

Phase four, the ground campaign, saw a rapid success. In February 1991, Iraqi forces were driven from Kuwait. They were out-generalled and out-fought by Coalition forces who benefited not only from superior technology but also from their ability to maintain a high-tempo offensive in executing a well-conceived plan that combined air and land strength. Allied fighting quality, unit cohesion, leadership and planning, and Iraqi deficiencies in each of these, all played a major role in ensuring victory. The technology attracted considerable interest due to the importance attached to precise bombardment. The Americans indeed employed satellite surveillance, Cruise missiles and guided bombs, as well as Patriot anti-missile missiles against Iraqi attacks.

The ground war began at 4 a.m. on 24 February 1991. The poorly led Iraqis had surrendered mobility by entrenching themselves to protect their conquest of Kuwait, a repetition of the methods they had followed during the Iran–Iraq War of 1980–8. Pessimistic predictions that the entrenchments would be difficult to take and that the Iraqis would force attritional warfare on the Coalition, causing heavy casualties – predictions which indeed ensured a large American provision of medical units[9] – were totally mistaken. While the Iraqis were attacked from the south on the direct route to Kuwait City, their right flank was outmanoeuvred by a rapid American advance through the desert to the west. This advance put pressure on the Iraqis when the outflanking American forces turned to attack them, destroying much of the Iraqi army on 27 February. The following morning, after 100 hours of non-stop combat, George H. W. Bush ordered a ceasefire. Over 50,000 Iraqis were dead, with 81,000 taken prisoner and nearly 4,000 tanks lost. In contrast, the Americans suffered 143 battle fatalities, thirty-three of them from 'friendly fire', a figure that reflected the difficulty of supplying in-time information about location.

Despite the rapid victory, the American doctrine of AirLand Battle had proved, like other military concepts, more difficult to execute in practice than to advance in theory and to train for, not least due to the problem of synchronising air and land forces under fast-moving combat conditions. Nevertheless, compared to earlier conflicts, such as the Linebacker II American air offensive on North Vietnam in December 1972, there was unified control over air operations, with a single air manager: the joint force air component commander. Moreover, target acquisition and accuracy were effective, and the pace of the air attack was maintained. Although the focus was on new technology, much of the weaponry was well established. Indeed, it was the bringing to higher, or optimal, performance of the latter that was very important. This, for example, was the case with tanks. The Gulf War provided opportunities to display the enhancement of the latter in recent years, notably as a result of the use of composite armour, high-performance engines and high first-shot-kill capability gun systems.

Some of the new technology performed very well. Cruise missiles successfully provided a new capability for surface warships, such as the battleship USS *Wisconsin,* demonstrating their capacity for littoral force projection. In contrast, some high-tech weaponry such as the British runway-cratering bombs and the American Patriot missile, did less well than was claimed at the time. In addition, important parts of the Allied military did not employ weaponry which was available. For example, the Americans used 9,300 precision-guided munitions, but most of their aircraft were not equipped, nor were their pilots trained for their use and instead employed unguided munitions, which made up 90 per cent of the aerial munitions employed. This use of unguided munitions was in spite of the precedent set by the extensive and effective use of precision-guided munitions in the Linebacker I and II campaigns in Vietnam in 1972. The situation was to be different in 2003. Similarly, in 1991, although the Americans had developed stealth aircraft, most of their planes lacked this expensive capability.[10]

The understandable focus on the American contribution to the Gulf War, which included over half a million military personnel, has led to an underestimation of the contribution of other states and indeed of the impact of the war on other states. For all those militaries that took part, the war raised issues of force projection, logistics and interoperability, although the last was eased by the experience of many in cooperation through NATO.[11] There was also an important contribution from states, principally Germany and Japan, who did not send troops into the combat zone but did provide financial support, indirect military help, or both, by freeing coalition forces for operations.

The varied politics of the war had important military implications. The conflict, for example, saw attacks on Israel by Iraqi Scud missiles, and, although they did not achieve their desired aim, of bringing Israel into the war and thus jeopardising Arab military and political support for the USA, especially from Saudi Arabia and Syria, the missiles underlined Israeli vulnerability. Concerned that Israel's deterrence had been lessened as a result of its inaction, the Israeli government wished to take reprisals on Iraq, but, aside from discouraging weather conditions, they were affected by American opposition to such action. The USA, however, did provide Israel with satellite information and Patriot missile batteries.

The need for the USA and Israel to counter the military and, even more, political threat from Scud missiles dramatised the implications of the spread of such weaponry. American anti-missile doctrine had long focused on Soviet intercontinental ballistic missiles, but the challenge posed by the Scuds indicated that short-range anti-missile defences and doctrine were also necessary and drew attention to the problems of relying on the Patriot missiles for that purpose.

More centrally to the Gulf War, the failure to keep military objectives and political goals in harmony helped ensure that the conflict did not lead to the hoped-for overthrow of Saddam Hussein. The American decision to end the offensive was taken in haste, in a war that was very high-tempo, without an adequate consideration of how to translate the outcome of the campaign into a durable post-war settlement. This failure was linked to military factors, specifically the persistence of 'friction' and 'fog'. At any rate, an inability to distinguish victory from the large-scale operational success which was obtained helped ensure that the wrong decisions were taken. The civilian leadership permitted the decision to end the war to be governed by military considerations, specifically the expulsion of Iraqi forces from Kuwait; but the major goal, in fact, was political: the need to create a stable post-war situation in the Gulf, the military preconditions for such stability being ultimately a political judgement.

It was not only with the benefit of hindsight that it became clear that the decision to end the war was taken too soon, jeopardising the prospect for victory: this was also apparent at the time. There were, however, concerns about the legal mandate and international backing for the liberation of Iraq (as opposed to Kuwait) and anxiety that overthrowing Saddam Hussein might lead to the dissolution of Iraq as the Shia rebelled in the south or, at least, could leave Iran too strong and thus challenge the balance of power in the Persian Gulf, as indeed was to happen in 2003. Nevertheless, whatever the benefit from liberating Kuwait and weakening Iraq in 1991, the end result was highly unfortunate. After the Coalition ceased its advance, Saddam was able to use his forces, particularly the Revolutionary Guard and its artillery and tanks (the army closest to him), to smash a rebellion in the south by the country's Shia majority, causing heavy casualties and destroying Shia shrines. This destruction was a key way of damaging Shia cohesion and demonstrating the regime's power. It corresponded to the destruction of churches and mosques in the conflicts in former Yugoslavia later in the decade.

In contrast, in Operation Provide Comfort, a multi-service, multinational task force, which was essentially a continuation of the Gulf War Coalition, protected the Kurds in northern Iraq from action by Saddam's forces. This protection was an important continuation to restraining Saddam and, in the longer term, to the liberation of Iraq from his control. The war was also followed by the long-term use of Allied air power in order to try to prevent Iraq from rebuilding its military, but this proved an expensive commitment which had only limited success – not least because policing Iraqi 'no-fly zones' was easier than influencing developments on the ground.[12] Furthermore, launched in response to the Iraqi refusal to allow in UN inspectors to assess its weapons programme, the Anglo-American Desert Fox bombing campaign in 1998 was not regarded as a success, although it has since been argued that it had an important effect on Iraqi decision-making.[13]

The wider political context for Iraq was not so much that of the Middle East but rather that of Europe, specifically the end of the Cold War with the collapse of the Soviet Union which was dissolved at the close of 1991 as the former republics of the Soviet Union became independent states. The end of the Cold War did not lead to the 'end of history' or the 'peace dividend', both of which were foretold by some of the more superficial commentators who believed that Soviet collapse represented a triumph for American-led democratic capitalism and that there would be no future clash of ideologies to destabilise the world. The military consequences, however, were significant. In what was a transformation in strategic affairs, the Western powers, led by the USA, were now able to intervene more frequently against states that earlier would otherwise have looked for Soviet support, not least because, aside from arms and military support, the Soviet Union would have vetoed supportive UN resolutions in the Security Council. Events in the UN did not match American expectations in 2003, but, whatever the situation there, the USA was now better able to give effect to its strength. This shift in context proved fatal to Saddam Hussein in both 1991 and 2003.

Moreover, in the 1990s, this greater opportunity for intervention was accompanied by a drive for such intervention. The established parameters within which peacekeeping was generally expected to take place, especially that conflict had already ended and that the government of the state in question accepted the deployment of peacekeepers, were interpreted increasingly generously, as seen with the use of terms such as 'peace support', 'peace-making' and 'peace-enforcement'. Interventionism, however, encountered the problem that the leading Western power, the USA, had an ambivalent relationship with the constraints of collective security, especially with the United Nations (UN), and not least with the notion of UN direction of operations involving American forces.

American force projection was not challenged by a revived Russia, the largest republic in the Soviet Union, because the collapse of the Soviet Union was not followed by a stronger Russia. Instead, it faced serious economic difficulties as the dismantling of the old command economy exposed the uncompetitive nature of much Soviet-era industry, while it proved difficult to establish effective monetary and fiscal mechanisms. Western loans were necessary in order to prevent a total collapse of Russia in the 1990s, and, even so, debt payments caused a severe crisis in 1998, leading to default and devaluation.

From 1989, moreover, Soviet (and then Russian) power collapsed in Eastern Europe, and garrisons were withdrawn. The last Russian troops left the former East Germany in 1994. Moreover, former Russian allies joined NATO: Poland, the Czech Republic and Hungary being the first to do so in 1997. The former East Germany had already become a member of NATO with German unification in 1990, a step that led to the dismantling of the *Volksarmee* and the incorporation of some of its members into the *Bundeswehr.* As an indication of the geopolitical potential of Communist forces in Eastern Europe, East German military *matériel* was illicitly shipped to Iraq in 1990 by members of the *Volksarmee.*

With Russian weakness, the arithmetic of deterrence, underlined as it was by the risk of mutually assured destruction, no longer discouraged overt Western intervention in the Third World. Indeed, in January 1994, the American and Russian leaders agreed not to target each other's states with their strategic nuclear weapons. The end of the Cold War also increased the number of potential allies for the West and thus deepened its logistical capability (leading, for example, to plans for bases in Romania and Bulgaria) and strengthened its capacity for force projection. At the same time, this capacity was put at the service of a mixture of regional objectives, and a universalist aspiration to secure a more benign world order, that posed serious challenges not only to Western military capability but also to related political goals.

In particular, there were acute issues of prioritisation between alternative commitments, and also of how best to devise sensible political missions that matched military capability and how best to organise and enhance the latter in order to secure missions. A variety of military devices and doctrines, such as American preparation for confronting two major regional crises simultaneously and American (from 1992) and British reconceptualisation of naval warfare towards littoral power projection, were important but did not address the issues of the sensible assessment of objectives and the political management of conflict.

The specifics, however, were, as is so often the case, less easy to cope with. From success in the Gulf War, attention usually turns to American failure in Somalia. That indeed is a key contrast that requires exposition, but it is one that is mishandled if the contrast is simply in terms of American success or failure. Instead, it is necessary to consider the particular nature of the Somali military and political environment, one that contrasted greatly with Iraq. If the latter, in 1991, was a weaker surrogate for the Soviet Union and an opponent for which the American military was prepared, neither was true of Somalia.

Moreover, American intervention in Somalia was in fact tangential to a bitter and lengthy period of conflict there. Following Somalia's failure in the Ogaden war with Ethiopia in 1977–8, a key episode in regional power politics and a largely overlooked Cold War conflict, a weaker President Siad Barre had faced growing opposition from clans which, increasingly, obtained heavier arms. In addition, the Somali National Movement mounted a serious challenge from 1978, although in 1988 the government was able to drive it from the northern towns it had seized, albeit causing heavy civilian casualties in the process. In 1989–90, other resistance movements further eroded Barre's position, full-scale civil war broke out, and Barre fled into exile in January 1991, mounting unsuccessful attempts to return that April, as well as in April and September 1992.

Somalia was increasingly split into areas uneasily controlled by clan factions, each of which deployed artillery and armoured vehicles, as well as the light lorries carrying heavy machine guns which were a distinctive feature of Somali warfare. These lorries were more generally used across much of North Africa, for example in Chad, enabling a bypassing of the meagre road network. Several of the Somali clans also made use of child fighters.

The UN intervened in Somalia in 1992 in order to bring humanitarian relief, although also to resolve immediate security problems. The UN forces, however, were inadequate to the latter task, and the ambiguity of the mission helped to lead to chaos.

The Americans, in Operation Restore Hope, initially provided 28,000 men of the 37,000 UN force, their advance guard arriving to great publicity. Mohamed Farrah Aidid, whose faction dominated the south of the dusty capital, Mogadishu, was a key local figure. The rivalry between Aidid and the Abgal subclan under Ali Mahdi Muhammad, which dominated northern Mogadishu, was an important backdrop to UN intervention as the UN force originally sent to Somalia was in part designed to help maintain a ceasefire between the two factions brokered by the UN in March 1992.

In May 1993, the scope of the UN forces expanded when, in pursuit of a secure environment, they were given the task of disarming the factions and controlling all heavy weapons. By then, the forces were 28,000 strong, including an American quick-reaction force. Aidid opposed this UN mission, and, on 5 June 1993, his men ambushed a Pakistani unit, killing twenty-four men. This urban ambush led the UN, supported by the USA, to move against Aidid, action which included mounting a helicopter gunship attack on 12 July. In an escalating crisis, attacks by Aidid on US troops in August led the American government to dispatch special-operations forces which were intended to capture hostile clan leaders, particularly Aidid.

On 3 October 1993, the American Task Force Ranger captured several Aidid supporters (but not Aidid) in a raid in Mogadishu but then met opposition, with two helicopters shot down. As a result, the Somalis that day gained the initiative on the ground, while the Americans were spread out and vulnerable. Evacuation needs became far more complex. Helicopters provided vital cover as well as dropping water, but the attempt to provide ground relief that day failed. In the clash that continued until the force was relieved by American, Pakistani and Malaysian troops early next day, the Americans suffered eighteen dead and eighty-three wounded, while about 500 Somalis were killed. Most of the Americans were successfully evacuated despite heavy odds, and several key Aidid supporters had been captured, but the operation was perceived as a failure by the Clinton government and an American population not prepared for losses and unclear about goals in Somalia. There had certainly been overconfidence on the part of government and commanders alike.[14]

In reaction to their losses, the Americans abandoned aggressive operations in Somalia, deciding, on 5 October 1993, to withdraw all American troops by the following March. This decision was seized on by Osama Bin Laden, the Saudi-born leader of the Islamicist terrorist movement al-Qaeda (The Base), to argue that the Americans could be forced to retreat as the Soviets had been from Afghanistan in 1988. This argument helped inspire Bin Laden's 'Declaration of War against the Americans Occupying the Land of the Two Holy Places', issued in August 1996. The Declaration called for the expulsion of American forces from Saudi Arabia, where their presence was a legacy of the Gulf War of 1990–1, and for the overthrow of what was seen as the pro-American Saudi government.

Most of the American troops left in March 1994, while the UN forces withdrew from Somalia in March 1995.[15] Faction-fighting continued, and the number of factions increased, as did civilian casualties. By 2003, the country was divided into about twenty-five warring fiefdoms, while clashes continued, and by 2008 Somalia was regarded as one of al-Qaeda's leading areas of operation. After 1994, no American combat troops were sent on peacekeeping missions to Africa. This was a policy that limited the options for international intervention during the Rwanda crisis (see pp. 49–50), and in 2003, when pressure built up for UN intervention in the mounting crisis in Congo, the American government made it clear that it would not send troops. Moreover, in Liberia, a state founded by America which was devastated by civil war, the Americans restricted themselves essentially to providing logistical support for Nigerian peacekeepers. American interests in sub-Saharan Africa had been directly attacked when al-Qaeda mounted truck-bomb attacks on American embassies in Nairobi and Dar es Salaam in 1998, but, in the aftermath of failure in Somalia, American military engagement with the continent remained limited.

More generally, in October 2007, Robert Gates, the Secretary of Defense, told the conference of the Association of the United States Army:

In the years following the Vietnam War, the Army relegated unconventional war to the margins of training, doctrine, and budget priorities . . . This approach may have seemed validated by ultimate victory in the Cold War and the triumph of Desert Storm. But it left the service unprepared to deal with the operations that followed: Somalia, Haiti, the Balkans, and more recently Afghanistan and Iraq – the consequences and costs of which we are still struggling with today.

The culture of the American military played a key role, as notions of self- and collective worth and institutional culture were closely bound up with regular warfare. Failure in Vietnam and Somalia encouraged this assessment. The equivalent counterpointing of regular and counter-insurgency with hard and soft power contributed to this, as the former was felt to be more masculine. There was also a linguistic tendency to regard regular warfare as real or true warfare, and irregular warfare, and thus COIN warfare, as a corruption that could, and should, be compartmentalised. In part, this approach drew on the reaction within the American military to the Vietnam War and the sense that failure there was a result of inappropriate tasking. The contrast with success in the 1991 Gulf War underlined this perception. Moreover, within the American army and elsewhere, there was uneasiness about the extent to which a stress on COIN warfare might lead to a diminished ability to engage successfully in regular warfare.

Failure in Somalia, however, did not prevent American action nearer home, where political sensitivities were stronger. In Operation Uphold Democracy in 1994, the USA sent 20,000 troops to Haiti in pursuit of a UN mandate to restore Jean-Bertrand Aristide, the President deposed by a military coup in 1991. This intervention was seen as a way to stop the flight of Haitian refugees to the USA and was an instance of the extent to which population movements helped prompt military actions, with, in this case, the pressures of domestic American politics against such immigration providing a key impetus.

In the event, Aristide's restoration was achieved by negotiation rather than force, although it proved difficult to make Haitian society conform to the goals of the subsequent US-dominated

UN peacekeeping mission, and the later history of Haiti was far from benign.[16] Indeed, the corruption and violence associated with the Aristide regime culminated with his overthrow in 2004. This overthrow was due to a domestic rising but was linked to American pressure on the regime and against the associated violence, a violence which, in turn, led to the deployment of American and French troops.

The peacekeeping and humanitarian support goals of the interventions in Haiti and Somalia were correctly described as low-intensity conflict, as any comparison with the wars against Iraq would demonstrate, but these interventions were still difficult and dangerous for the troops involved, and the mission culture that stemmed from the nature of peacekeeping added to the difficulty. It proved hard to secure adequate and timely intelligence, both military and political, and to bring the two into line, while the unpreparedness of the American military for operating in urban environments was revealed in Mogadishu. The relative ease of Operation Joint Cause, the rapid overthrow of the regime of the drug-dealing General Noriega in Panama in December 1989, proved no real preparation for the problems, both military and political, of Mogadishu in 1993. As a result of the fate of the latter intervention, Operation Uphold Democracy in Haiti was supported by adequate force. Moreover, it was no accident that American defence expenditure rose in the early 1990s.

Yet, as always, the adequacy of force depended largely on the political context and on the skill with which the mission was crafted. The American preference for being prepared for warfighting led to a practice of overwhelming force that worked in Panama and Haiti. This emphasis differed from the British preference for minimum necessary force, as well, more seriously, as from the necessity for long-term commitment focused on nation-building.

Action of a very different type characterised the former Soviet Union, as competing interests sought to direct the fate of successor republics or, indeed, to ensure, or prevent, their dissolution. Thus, the army of the newly independent Georgian state used force in an unsuccessful attempt to resist separatism by the Muslim province of Abkhazia, but the latter received crucial Russian diplomatic and military assistance. More than 200,000 Georgians (over half of the population of Abkhazia) were driven from their homes. A Russian 'peacekeeping' force is still there in order to pre-empt any possible action by Georgia and to show that Russia can protect its protégés. The lesson was driven home in 2008 when Russia successfully intervened against Georgia in order to protect separatist protégés in South Ossetia.

In addition, following the collapse of the Soviet Union, the newly independent republics of Armenia and Azerbaijan fought, in 1992–4, over control of the region of Nagorno-Karabakh, a struggle won by Armenia.[17] Only 1 million Azerbaijanis became refugees. There was also a bitter clan-based civil war in Tajikistan between 1992 and 1997 in which about 50,000 people were killed. There, a 25,000-strong, Russian-dominated, peacekeeping force helped ensure the defeat of the southern groups, including Muslim fundamentalists, that had contested the dominance of northerners, although the resolution was not peace but rather a guerrilla struggle. Pressure to end the conflict in 1997 in part reflected concern that Taliban success in Afghanistan would be followed by Taliban intervention in Central Asia. At a smaller scale, Uzbeks and Meskhetian Turks fought in the Ferghana Valley of Uzbekistan. Further west, the 'Trans-Dniester Republic', supported by the forces of the former Soviet 14th Army, sought to break away from the newly independent republic of Moldova.

The USA and other Western powers benefited from the collapse of the Soviet Union to establish a degree of military cooperation with some of the successor states, a key instance of the more widespread relationship between military-assistance programmes and political, ideological and economic change, if not transformation. For example, from 1994, Ukraine's military was given American money under military cooperation programmes, and some of its officers were trained in the USA.[18] Georgia also turned to the West. Russia, however, bitterly opposed NATO expansion.

The deficiencies of the Soviet military were to be cruelly demonstrated in the accidental sinking of the nuclear submarine *Kursk* in 2000, which dramatised the decline of Russian naval power. The Soviet navy had become the second largest naval power, but it became increasingly obsolescent in the 1980s and 1990s as it proved impossible to sustain the cost of new units, and in the 1990s the navy was gravely affected by the break-up of the Soviet Union. This break-up was particularly important in the case of the Black Sea naval base of Sevastopol, which came under the authority of Ukraine and was affected by the tension between pro- and anti-Russian movements there.

More profound problems were revealed in the Caucasus, where the Russians encountered serious difficulties from Muslim separatist movements which were able to rely on considerable popular support, in part because of a tradition of ethnic strife. The Chechen Republic of the Russian Federation was a centre of separatism, and in 1991 it declared its independence from Russia. The Chechen President, Dzhokhar Dudayev, represented an interesting combination of military traditions. He had risen through the Soviet air force, becoming its first Chechen general and commanding strategic nuclear bombers based in Estonia. In Afghanistan in the 1980s, Dudayev had developed a new bombing strategy against the Mujahidin, the Afghans resisting Soviet control. Yet, he had also come to be impressed by the nationalism of the Afghans and Estonians and adopted the guerrilla tactics of the former. In Chechnya, Dudayev issued a decree giving every man the right to bear arms. In 1993, he used National Guard units to dissolve a provisional supreme council appointed by Boris Yeltsin, the Russian President.

Yeltsin, unwilling to accept separatism, not least because of oil in the area and his fear of the consequences in terms of encouraging separatism in nearby areas of Russia, responded by invading Chechnya in December 1994. The previous month, a covert attack on the capital, Grozny, in support of pro-Russian groups fighting Dudayev's supporters had failed. In December, the Russians deployed nearly 24,000 troops, including 4,700 from the Ministry of Internal Affairs Forces (a key paramilitary force), as well as eighty tanks and ninety helicopters. Many, however, were poorly trained. Russian forces captured Grozny in January 1995 after lengthy and difficult operations in which they employed devastating firepower, especially intensive artillery barrages and bombing, in a city of near half a million people. This city provided a terrain ideally suited to well-motivated opponents; some Chechens were former Soviet soldiers who understood urban fighting tactics. Rocket-propelled grenades were employed effectively in attacks on Soviet armoured vehicles, while ambushes were frequent. The Russians were eventually successful, but many of their opponents escaped.

Brutality and intransigence, however, encouraged resistance which the Russians were unable to crush. In 1996, they withdrew (and the Chechens occupied Grozny) under a peace agreement in order to strengthen Yeltsin's position in a presidential campaign. The 1994–6 campaigns revealed the deficiencies of the badly led, badly equipped, badly motivated and under-strength Russian forces. Not least among these deficiencies was the lack of appropriate training and doctrine for COIN warfare, although it is also necessary to emphasise large Chechen numbers and the extent to which the Chechens, though poorly disciplined, were well armed (if short of ammunition) and determined.[19] Many indeed had also been trained through conscription in the Soviet army. The rebels were also able to receive support from across the region's borders.

In turn, the Russian preference in Chechnya for large-scale firepower reflected the dominance in their doctrine and practice of preparations for conventional war with the West,[20] while, more seriously, the Russians appeared to have no response other than force and yet could not use that effectively, nor really afford it. The Russians added to the usual problems affecting COIN policies, the difficulty of transforming these policies into peacekeeping; they failed at both.

The renewed Russian attack on Chechnya in 2000 was provoked by Chechen moves into neighbouring Daghestan and by explosions in Moscow blamed on Chechen terrorists. In Daghestan, about 600 members of the Wahhabi sect, some of them Daghestanis, but many not, sought both to destroy Russian power and also to coerce the population, most of whom were moderate Muslims. Control of the villages was contested, as the rebels were not strong enough to seize the capital, Makhachkala. The rival forces essentially operated in different environments: the rebels on paths, the mechanised Russian forces on roads, a long-standing pattern of insurrectionary and COIN warfare.

In practice, the explosions in Moscow, and possibly even the fighting in Daghestan, may have reflected the direct or indirect intervention of the Russian secret police, whose influence can be compared with that of the Inter-Services Intelligence (ISI) agency in Pakistan. The renewed attack on Chechnya certainly reflected the determination of a secret-police product, Yeltsin's prime minister, and eventual successor, Vladimir Putin, to assert control, and this looked towards the use of force against Georgia in 2008.

The Russian campaign led to the fall of Grozny in January 2000 but indicated similar military deficiencies. As with other forces battling insurgency, the Russians suffered from the problem of inadequate intelligence, which reflected the limitations of surveillance in such contexts. In such a situation, later seen with Coalition forces in Iraq and in Afghanistan, there was an over-reliance on firepower responses, often poorly directed. Guerrilla opposition in Chechnya, including suicide bombings there and elsewhere in Russia, continued, and, in response, the Russians mounted raids on guerrilla areas and seized suspected Chechens. Opposition was firmest in the mountainous south.[21] Chechnya, however, did not define what was a spreading pattern of violent Muslim opposition, especially elsewhere in the northern Caucasus. This spread even led to concern about the stability of Russia vis-à-vis a widespread and sustained terrorist movement.[22] The differential birth rates of Muslims and non-Muslims made this issue more acute.

The fall of the Soviet Union also played an important role in the myth-making that helped encourage consolidate Osama Bin Laden's al-Qaeda movement. Drawing on Egyptian and Saudi Arabian fundamentalist theology and Islamicist political culture – and on Saudi money – Bin Laden's movement was a rejection of the West, of modernity and of what were perceived to be the secular allies of both in the Muslim world, as well as an aspect of deep-rooted tensions, for example Sunni hostility towards Shias. In opposition to the West, al-Qaeda drew on a widespread anxiety, frustration and anger, and on a rejectionism that was not interested in debate or on what outsiders would perceive as a rational assessment. Believing in mission and inevitability, Bin Laden sought to fit events into a panorama demonstrating the truth of his prospectus.

The collapse of the Soviet Union proved a key episode as this was presented as arising from the Soviet failure in Afghanistan, a failure in which future members of al-Qaeda had played a role, including Bin Laden. Supposedly the war in Afghanistan demonstrated that faith could overcome an advanced power.[23] In practice, this was a serious misjudgement of the relationship between failure in Afghanistan and Soviet collapse. The latter collapse was largely due to the interaction of Gorbachev's policies with nationalism both in Eastern Europe and within the Soviet Union. Moreover, Bin Laden greatly underplayed the role of Western, especially American, support in Afghanistan, notably in the provision of missiles able to curtail the role of Soviet air superiority (although he was keen to acquire such technology for his own use), and also did not note the extent to which the Soviets only devoted a relatively small percentage of their military resources to the Afghan war.[24] Instead, the Soviet military in the 1980s focused on confrontation with NATO and China.

While the fall of the Soviet Union led to conflict in the Caucasus, the disintegration of Yugoslavia in 1991 into its constituent republics had the same effect in the Balkans. A federal state held together earlier by its Communist dictator, Josip Broz Tito, Yugoslavia was divided between ethnic groups, most prominently Serbs and Croats, that sought independence for the areas they dominated and pursued the widest possible definition of the latter. As, and after, the Yugoslav state collapsed, Franjo Tuđman, the authoritarian president of Croatia from 1991 to 1999, used nationalism to provide both identity and rationale for his power, and the same was true of Serbia under Slobodan Milošević. Moreover, in 1991, in the far north of the country, about 70,000 men out of a population of only 2 million Slovenes mobilised in order to resist attempts to prevent Slovene independence, and the Serb-dominated Yugoslav army did not push the issue to widespread conflict.

In contrast, the army made a far greater effort against Croatia, which, unlike Slovenia, had a border with Serbia and also contained a large Serb minority. This war, which began in the Krajina region in the summer of 1991, with bitter fighting that autumn over the city of Vukovar, spilled over into Bosnia. This was a republic of Yugoslavia which was ethnically mixed, with large Croat (Catholic), Serb (Orthodox) and Bosniak (Bosnian Muslim) populations. Suffering from both Croat and Serbian expansion, each of the communities in Bosnia formed an army. The Bosnian Serbian and Bosnian Croat forces cooperated with the armies of Serbia and Croatia, pursuing their own and joint objectives.

The conflicts in Yugoslavia were brutal, but also limited. War there involved demonstration and negotiation, a politics by military means which were intensively political, a mixture of sudden and brief brutality with truces and convoluted strategies of diplomacy. Fighting in the capital, Sarajevo, from 1992 to 1995 included high-intensity street fighting but served as much as a tool for propaganda as for military advantage. Bosnian Serb bombardments of the city were aimed at political or psychological targets rather than at military objectives that could help capture the city.[25] At the same time, the disruption was acute, and most of the Bosnian population became refugees, fleeing to areas under sympathetic control or abroad.

Western intervention to end a conflict on Europe's doorstep was weakened by a combination of European weakness and American reluctance. The latter was not only from President Clinton but also from an American military leadership concerned about mission creep and the problems of fighting insurgent forces in difficult terrain. The United Nations Protection Force, created in April 1992 in response to the outbreak of civil war in Bosnia, proved too weak and restricted to maintain order and, in particular, to restrain the aggression of the Bosnian Serbs. NATO launched its first combat action, air strikes, in 1994, but they were limited in number and affected by restrictive rules of engagement. Despite this, settlements were eventually imposed in Bosnia in 1995 and in Kosovo in 1999, at the expense of the expansionism and ethnic aggression of a Serbian regime that unsuccessfully looked for Russian sponsorship. The West played a major role, with 3,515 sorties flown and 100 Cruise missiles fired (as well as artillery used against the Serbs), in Operation Deliberate Force in 1995, the first large-scale NATO combat mission.[26]

Yet, the ability of Serbia's opponents, especially the Croats, to organise military forces capable of opposing the Serbs in the field was more important in preventing Serb victory, and then in taking war to the Serbs. This ability was seen in the autumn of 1995 when the Croats and the Bosnian Muslims, who had been brought together in 1994, in part by American pressure, were able to mount successful offensives against the Bosnian Serbs, the Croats overrunning first western Slavonia and then the Krajina, while the Bosnian Serbs were driven from central Bosnia. The attacking forces, which were assisted by a private military company, Military Professional Resources Incorporated, may have numbered 200,000 men. Combined with NATO air attack and diplomatic pressure, these offensives pushed the Serbs into accepting the Dayton Peace Agreement on 21 November 1995.

The brutal slaughter of civilians by the Serbs (and, to a lesser extent, by their opponents) was an all-too-familiar feature of conflict in much of the modern world and reflected the extent to which ethnic groups were seen as the units of political strength, and thus as targets. In July 1995, the Bosnian Serbs murdered about 7,000 unarmed Muslim males in Srebrenica, which had been designated a safe zone by UN representatives whose peace-keeping force was too weak and too focused on self-preservation to prevent the massacre. The restrictive nature of the instructions under which UN forces operated was also a serious issue. It became clear that humanitarian interventions required a very robust military dimension, able to provide effective protection and to ensure coercion.

Among the combatants in the former Yugoslavia, what was termed 'ethnic cleansing' – the expulsion of members of an ethnic group – was more common than massacres. 'Ethnic cleansing' was generally associated with the Serbs but was also used by the Croats, for example against Serbs in Krajina.[27] Croat action does not excuse Serb actions, but it helps explain the paranoia that characterised Serbian policy-makers.

In turn, such action against civilians led to pressure on outside powers to adapt existing views on peacekeeping in order to adopt a proactive policy of peace enforcement focused on humanitarian goals. This new priority overcame earlier hesitations about military action.[28] The NATO Implementation Force (IFOR) sent in to ensure compliance with the Drayton Accords was more powerful than the UN force had been. It included 57,000 troops, 20,000 of them Americans. In December 1996, IFOR became the Stabilization Force. This was a successful deployment, and fighting markedly declined.[29]

Humanitarian goals were central to liberal internationalism, which became more pronounced as a theme in Western policy in the 1990s. Such intervention, however, presupposed that success could be readily obtained, and belief in this intervention relied on the notion of a clear capability gap between the two sides. Indeed, from the humanitarian perspective, the forces of good had to be successful in order to avoid the suffering that could result from military operations. These suppositions helped explain the difficulties faced by Anglo-American representatives when they discussed massive Iraqi civilian casualties during and after the war of 2003.

Later in the 1990s, in order to suppress separatist demands, as well as to destroy support for the Kosovo Liberation Army, which had begun attacks on the police in 1996, the Serbs also used the tactics of ethnic cleansing in Kosovo, part of Serbia with a majority ethnic-Albanian and Muslim population where the Serbian regime had long resisted demands for autonomy. The Western response over Kosovo was coercive diplomacy, which, in 1999, became a forceful humanitarian mission, Operation Allied Force. Costing over 3 billion dollars, the resulting seventy-seven-day bombing and Cruise-missile assault by American, British and French forces (and other NATO countries), however, was far less effective than Operation Deliberate Force had been in 1995. President Clinton, nevertheless, made public his unwillingness to commit land forces as well. Yet, the air assault helped lead in 1999 to the Serb withdrawal and acceptance of a ceasefire, which was followed by the establishment of a NATO peacekeeping force headed by Britain, France, Germany, Italy and the USA. Thereafter, the continuing isolation of Serbia, in a form of economic and financial warfare, contributed to an erosion of support for Milošević and his fall in the face of Serbian popular action in 2000.

In 1999, George Robertson, the British Secretary of State for Defence (and later Secretary General of NATO), publicly scorned commentators who warned about the difficulty of winning the Kosovo conflict by air power alone, and also about the contrast between output (bomb and missile damage) and outcome. However, the use of air power in Bosnia had already amply demonstrated the problems of managing an air assault when the alliance responsible was divided about its application. The air attack in 1999 suffered the loss of only two aircraft, but the subsequent Serbian withdrawal from Kosovo revealed that NATO estimates of the damage inflicted by air attack, for example to Serb tanks, had been considerably exaggerated. The Serbs benefited in practice from the limitations of Allied intelligence information, and its serious consequences for Allied targeting, and from the severe impact of the weather on Allied air operations, a large number of which were cancelled or affected. As a result, despite 10,000 NATO strike sorties, the Serbs, employing simple and inexpensive camouflage techniques that took advantage of the terrain and the wooded cover, preserved most of their equipment. Furthermore, the air offensive had not prevented the large-scale expulsion of Kosovars from their homes, and this expulsion badly compromised the success of the NATO operation. Indeed, the Serbian ethnic-cleansing campaign, Operation Horseshoe, increased as the air attack mounted.

The Serb withdrawal in 1999 may have owed more to a conviction, based in part on Russian information and the build-up of American forces in Albania, that a NATO land attack was imminent, as well as to the withdrawal of Russian support, rather than to the air offensive, although French, German and, eventually, American rejection of British pressure for such an invasion indicated their doubts of its feasibility. Indeed, a land attack on Kosovo faced serious logistical challenges and was dependent on the willingness of neighbouring countries to provide access and bases. This lack of willingness, especially on the part of Greece, which was unwilling to permit the use of the port of Thessaloniki, contributed to the mistake of not preparing adequate options in the event of the air offensive failing. Albania represented a far less attractive option as a base, not least for reasons of transport infrastructure, logistical capability and invasion routes into Kosovo.

The Kosovo crisis suggested that air power would be most effective as part of a joint strategy, and, indeed, ground and air threats were not totally separate: the eventual threat to the Serbs on the ground from a NATO invasion made their forces vulnerable to air attack, as it made dispersal, rather than concentration, a less viable proposition. Moreover, although the damage to the Serbian army from air attack was limited, the devastation of Serbia's infrastructure, in the shape of bridges, factories and electrical power plants, was important, not least because it affected the financial interests of the elite as well as its morale and the functioning of the economy. Thus, there was a marked contrast between the limited tactical and operational, but possibly more effective strategic, impact of air power.

The issue of the legitimate use of force was prominently raised in 1999. The majority of the Kosovars expelled returned to their homes in the wake of the Serbian withdrawal. Their return was key to the claims of 'success' for the NATO operation.[30] Kosovo, however, then saw much violence against Serbian civilians by ethnic Albanians. Moreover, Kosovo, like Bosnia, remained tense, and in 2004 there were murderous anti-Serbian riots in the Kosovo town of Mitrovica. As with Macedonia in 1999–2001, the perspective on Western intervention varies greatly.[31]

In Macedonia (the Greeks insist that it is termed the Former Yugoslav Republic of Macedonia) in 2001, the interaction of ethnic grievance, political demonisation and security problems led to the escalation of a 'semi-criminal battle in a lawless region' into an insurrection by the National Liberation Army, a new ethnic Albanian guerrilla group that looked to Kosovo. This insurrection, however, was checked by a NATO-backed counter-attack before a political agreement was negotiated. In the fighting, the Macedonians used attack helicopters and artillery but also found that they could only achieve so much, notably in the fighting around Aračinovo in June 2001.[32]

The use and experience of Western military power in the 1990s offered different conclusions. On the whole, there was a major burst of optimism about Western prospects, which drew on the combination of the collapse of the Soviet Union, the rapid defeat of Iraq and belief in an RMA. The major growth of the

American economy was also very important. Benefiting from the important structural reforms of the late 1970s and 1980s, which, in part, entailed a move away from earlier corporatist practices, and from the speedy diffusion of most efficient economic practices and investment, the American economy grew rapidly. International trade liberalisation in the 1990s was also important. In contrast to claims about likely decline, most prominently by Paul Kennedy in 1988, America's position in the global economy was indicated by the substantial rise in its shape of global exports – from 15.7 per cent in 1993 to 17.7 per cent in 1999 – and that in the period of major growth in world trade.[33] There was also a rise in the American percentage of the world's gross domestic product (GDP) and of America's contribution to the increasing gap in per-capita income between the West and the rest. The greater potency of American ballistic missiles offered a hard-edged demonstration of this power and wealth. The Trident II D-5 sea-launched missile, deployed from 1990, considerably increased the accuracy of such missiles, while the ability to use the W88 warhead with the missile increased their yield and, therefore, capability.[34]

Within sections of the 'international community', especially among jurists, there was also a more critical attitude towards the use of force. It was as if bellicosity was reformulated, away from being a justified aspect of the sovereignty of individual states. Instead, bellicosity was seen as a problem in others, and, in response, there was emphasis on a different bellicosity, one that was a necessity in pursuit of the maintenance of international order and the implementation of systemic norms. This view provided the background to ideas about the desirability of interventionist warfare. These ideas are not new (and some, to an extent, are the secularisation of earlier religious ideas about conflict between co-religionists), but their application is very much so. It is, however, unclear whether these allegedly normative ideas help us in understanding or in overcoming the values of opponents for whom compromise is unacceptable, force necessary, and even desirable, and war crucial to identity and self-respect.

Moreover, at the same time, there were signs of limitations in Western military effectiveness and capability. The setback in Somalia in 1993 and the delay in Kosovo in 1999 were both indicative of wider problems. The Israelis, for example, found it difficult to suppress opposition in southern Lebanon and in the occupied Palestinian territories. In 1987, the intifada, a rebellion against Israeli rule in occupied territories, and specifically against the pace of Israeli settlement on the West Bank (Palestine west of the River Jordan), began with stone-throwing crowds challenging Israeli authority. The intifada was to underline the weakness of imposed political settlements in the Middle East, where the bulk of any population felt alienated, and also to expose the limitations of regular troops in the face of popular resistance. The Israeli military found it difficult to deal with what was to them a novel form of warfare, one far less welcome than conventional conflict with regular Arab armies. The Oslo Agreement of 1993 and the subsequent creation of a Palestinian autonomous territory under Yasser Arafat was to fail to prevent a resumed escalation of conflict in the 2000s.

In southern Lebanon, Hizbullah, a Shia guerrilla force, offered a stronger opposition to Israeli pressure than that mounted earlier by the guerrillas of the Palestinian Liberation Organization and Syrian regulars. Willing to take casualties, Hizbullah enjoyed Iranian support and was able to respond tactically to Israeli advantages, not least using surface-to-air missiles against Israeli air power. In Israeli attacks on Hizbullah forces in April 1996, the use of advanced technology, such as American Bell AH-1 Cobra helicopter gunships by the Israelis and of Soviet Katyusha rockets by their opponents, indicated the extent to which modern weapons systems were widely employed. The remarks of a Hizbullah spokesman that month are interesting: 'Do not say because we are weaker we should give in. Israel is not so strong. Look at the Vietnamese. Did they stop because America was stronger?' The spokesman was guarded by a fighter carrying an American M16 assault rifle.[35]

The problems of Western military power were particularly relevant to the gap between output and outcome and were not really related to a failure to maintain military strength, but the latter was also notable, not least in affecting the number of operations that could be mounted. Under President Bill Clinton (1993–2001), the American military was cut by a third and weapons procurement was reduced. Operational pressures, however, mounted – in large part due to unforeseen circumstances. For example, in 1999, the USA sent the sole aircraft carrier permanently assigned to the Pacific to the Mediterranean in order to contribute to the pressure on Serbia during the Kosovo crisis.

American force reductions made it increasingly likely that a major commitment would be launched with inadequate strength and/or would entail coalition resources. President George H. W. Bush's intention that the USA would be able to launch two Desert Storm-scale (1991 Gulf War) operations concurrently had to be abandoned, which led to pressure for greater effectiveness from smaller forces and also to concern about the ability to call on allies, and indeed about the gap between their military effectiveness and that of the USA, a gap that was held to threaten interoperability. Yet, there were (and remain) tensions between the external constraints that alliance policy-making entails and the nature of political culture in the USA, which tends to be hostile to compromise with foreign powers. American politicians and public opinion instinctively think in unilateral, and not multilateral, terms.

Pressure for greater effectiveness was in part a matter of the ideas (and ideology) summed up by the RMA, but there was also a more general sense about the need for military development to reflect different goals after the Cold War. This process was to be termed 'Transformation', but it was not limited to the policies subsequently described with that term. In part, there was a continuation of the inclination of the military (non-American as well as American) in the 1980s for more flexible structures as well as doctrine and operational planning that stressed mobility, but there were also important developments.

In the early 1990s, the American army's interest in employing information technology to enhance situational awareness was linked to a stress on agility and flexibility. The concept, Force XXI, sought to network battlefield information systems. To test the concept, a division-size experimental force was designated in December 1994 and adapted accordingly. In the Advanced Warfighting Experiment in 1997, a digitised task force was tested against a conventional opponent. This test proved more successful than the brigade-scale test carried out in 1994. The latter had revealed a lack of familiarity with new computerised equipment as well as the absence of the tactics necessary to exploit new capabilities.

In the late 1990s, the concept changed to the Army After Next Project. In place of adapting information technology to existing systems, there was a focus in the American army on a new generation of weapon systems, which were to be ready by 2025. The emphasis was on being able to respond rapidly to all circumstances, and, to that end, a 'Strike Force' was created to test the potential for rapid deployment of a force able to take the initiative. Pushing forward by Eric Shinseki, who became Chief of Staff in the army in 1999, this also entailed a broad front improvement including different logistical structures and an ability to function jointly with the other military services. Rapid deployment at a distance entailed airlift, and this need encouraged the development of smaller, lighter fighting vehicles which could be used to equip light infantry units. The plan was to be able to field a combat-ready brigade anywhere in the world in ninety-six hours and a division in 120 hours, a key enhancement in American capability and one that contrasted with the situation in 1990 when Iraq invaded Kuwait. The emphasis in American army planning now was on the brigade as the key unit, rather than the division; and this emphasis looked towards the decision, taken in 2003, to convert the army into a modular, brigade-based force.[36] The Stryker, an eight-wheeled medium-weight armoured vehicle, became the platform of choice, providing a mobile, armour-protected combat system, and with each vehicle able to connect with all the information systems serving the unit. A sense of greater effectiveness was to be derived from the comparison between the difficulties experienced in Mogadishu when trying to rescue two downed helicopters and the far less costly experience of a Stryker unit facing a similar task at Tal Afar in Iraq on 4 September 2004.[37]

The relationships between effectiveness, expenditure and foreign policy were indirect, but, under Clinton, there was a caution about policy in the Middle East that contrasted with the understandably more assertive and bellicose position under his successor in the far more threatening situation after the terrorist attacks on 11 September 2001. Under Clinton, threats to Saddam Hussein were not matched by action, while the challenge posed by Muslim terrorism (meaning Islamicist terrorism not terrorism representative of all or many Muslims) was not adequately met.

Cruise-missile strikes, however, were launched against terrorist bases in Afghanistan and Sudan in 1998, strikes of which the Republicans were sharply critical, and ironically so given the subsequent War on Terror. Mounted in response to al-Qaeda attacks on American embassies, the launching of these seventy-nine Cruise missiles represented an impressive display of force, but not one that stopped the terrorists. Indeed, Osama Bin Laden, the Saudi Arabian head of al-Qaeda, was able to raise funds by selling missiles that did not detonate to the Chinese, who were interested in cutting-edge American military technology. The failure of these attacks was a small part of a much wider inability to understand what was going on in the Muslim world, or indeed, the complex relationship between cause and effect.[38]

The reliance on Cruise missiles in 1998, as that on air power against Iraq that year (see p. 18), reflected at once the potential it brought for action without having to commit ground forces and yet also the hesitation about committing such forces that the Americans had also shown in the Balkans over Bosnia and were to show over Kosovo in 1999. Although it proved easy to blame such hesitation on a reluctant public lacking resolve, in practice there were powerful military and governmental factors that encouraged a disinclination to send ground forces, not least the army's unwillingness to become involved in a mission without apparent end and unless they had clear goals and readily apparent superiority, an unwillingness that drew on the legacy of Vietnam as well as on the unsuccessful intervention in Beirut in the 1980s and in Mogadishu. This attitude, which was dominant in American military thinking, was to pose problems in the aftermath of the Iraq invasion of 2003. It led to a focus on an attempt to use kinetic force in order to settle problems rather than on a need to think about what each mission entailed.

At the same time, prior to the al-Qaeda attacks in 2001, there were already signs of American concern about a more dangerous world order, signs that contrasted with optimism earlier in the 1990s. The *Strategic Assessment 1999* issued by the Institute for National Strategic Studies of the National Defense University commented on strengthened and hostile Sino-Russian ties, and later added:

> Of the three U.S. strategic goals – security, economic prosperity, and democracy – the last two have received considerable emphasis in recent years. This pattern reflects a belief that global security affairs have been stable enough to permit an emphasis on the world economy and democratic enlargement. Dangerous international trends now suggest that managing security affairs will need to be given attention and priority in the coming years. Pursuing economic progress and democracy will be difficult, unless security goals are first attained.[39]

The run-down of the military was taken further in Western Europe where there were significant cuts in the percentage of national wealth and government revenues spent on the armed forces. In Germany in 1999, this dropped to 1.5 per cent of GDP; leading to public complaints from the American Defense Secretary. There was also a reluctance to serve in the German military: 40–45 per cent of Germans who were drafted opted for social service, for example as paramedics. Moreover, as far as France was concerned, the capability of the Force d'Action Rapide in the Gulf War of 1991 was affected by the inability to demand that conscripts serve there. This problem encouraged the abandonment of conscription in France, and, in 1996, the decision was taken to professionalise totally the armed forces. In Spain, in 1993, when 118,000 of the 146,000-strong army were conscripts, the government decided that it could not contribute a brigade to the UN forces in Bosnia, as conscripts could not be expected to serve there and there were insufficient regulars. At that stage, most Spanish men of draft age never went into uniform. In 1999, Carlo Scognamiglio, the Italian Defence Minister, warned that Italy would be unable to guarantee its own security, let alone meet its foreign peacekeeping obligations, unless the number of professional soldiers was doubled from 25,000 to 50,000. He blamed Italy's falling birth rate and a liberal law on conscription allowing people to opt out of military service as conscientious objectors. In 2008, the newly elected Berlusconi government decided to deploy 3,000 troops from the 108,000-strong Italian army for six months on joint patrols with the police in nine cities, while troops were also to be used in sixteen cities in order to guard immigrant detention centres.

The state of the European militaries led to concern both there and in the USA where there were particular worries about interoperability with the Americans within NATO and also about the degree of European resolve. These concerns lay behind the political tensions that were to be far more manifest at the time of the Iraq War in 2003. The same was true of Canada, which cut its defence expenditure in the 1990s and refused to participate in the Iraq War. By 2007, Canada spent about 1.1 per cent of its GDP on the military, compared to about 2.6 per cent for France and over 3.9 per cent for the USA. Canada's full-time regular force was 62,000 strong, with another 25,000 in the reserves.

In part, differences between the USA and Western Europe reflected not only differing positions in the international order but also contrasting recent histories. The domestic logics of military power were pertinent, not only the location of this power in specific national political cultures but also the need for this power to maintain internal stability. This need was readily apparent with the British army in Northern Ireland. In contrast, the American military did not need to devote much effort to this task, although, in 1992, the deficiencies of the National Guard in responding to riots in Los Angeles led the Governor of California to request federal troops. Four thousand soldiers and marines were deployed, while the National Guard units there were federalised. This deployment led to a sharp decrease in levels of violence. The Los Angeles riots as a whole led to fifty-four deaths, 2,328 injuries and more than 900 million dollars of property damage.[40]

Capability and effectiveness do not exist in a vacuum. Before continuing the discussion of conflicts in which Western powers played the key role, it is necessary to turn to a different account of warfare in the 1990s, one in which the West had a role, but indirectly and without supplying the central narrative.

CHAPTER 3

SIGNS OF DIFFERENCE, 1990–2000

As with the situation prior to 1990, for example with the Iran–Iraq war, it would be misleading to ignore the number of conflicts between 'Third World' forces. Some of these, as in Somalia and Afghanistan, provided the background for Western intervention, but they are of significance for more than that. Furthermore, the process by which the Taliban seized power in most of Afghanistan in 1996 (see p. 58) is rather more indicative of post-1990 conflict than the American intervention in that country from 2001. Conflict between 'Third World' forces took a number of forms, ranging from regular warfare across front lines to insurrections, ethnic conflict, terrorism and coups. Most of this conflict occurred in Africa, but there were also important instances in Latin America, Asia and Oceania.

Some of the wars were continuations of Cold War conflicts, which was particularly true of Angola and El Salvador. Although the 1988 ceasefire in Angola was followed by the prompt departure of South African forces and, in 1991, by that of the Cubans who had fought on behalf of the Soviet-backed MPLA (Movimento Popular de Libertação de Angola; Popular Movement for the Liberation of Angola) government, the 1989 ceasefire between the government and the American-supported UNITA (União Nacional para a Independência Total de Angola; National Union for the Total Independence of Angola) movement speedily collapsed. This led to an upsurge in conflict, a fresh bout of diplomacy and a peace in 1991 that only lasted until UNITA rejected the results of the 1992 election.

In El Salvador, the Americans backed the government against the Farabundo/Marti National Liberation Front (FMLN). While the Cold War was fading in Europe, it continued in El Salvador, with a large-scale FMLN offensive in November 1989. This offensive took over part of the capital, San Salvador, for a week, but could not touch off a popular uprising.

Equally, the failure of the government of El Salvador to prevent the offensive led its American sponsors to press for negotiations which eventually, in 1992, bore fruit with a settlement under which the FMLN translated its activism to civilian politics. Its guerrillas were disbanded, and, in the elections of 1994, the FMLN became the largest opposition party, following this up, as a result of the 2000 elections, by becoming the largest parliamentary party. Similarly, in Nicaragua, where the civil war was brought to an end in 1990–4, the Sandinistas won power as a result of the 2006 elections.

These and other conflicts, however, had origins and a course that were not defined by the Cold War, however much the latter might have helped lead to foreign sponsorship.[1] The extent to which the Cold War was not central was seen in Africa. Thus, in the Horn of Africa, there was a centuries-old rivalry between the Ethiopians, who lived in the mountainous interior, and the Eritreans and Somalis who lived on the coast. This rivalry was fuelled by contrasting religious and ethnic constructions. In 1993, Ethiopia eventually conceded independence to Eritrea after a long secessionist movement in which the Ethiopian position had finally collapsed in 1991. This collapse was in part because of the fall of the brutal left-wing Mengistu regime in Ethiopia in the face of successful opposition by the Ethiopian People's Revolutionary Democratic Front and the Tigray People's Liberation Front. The Tigrayan leader, Meles Zenawi, became President of Ethiopia.

Similarly, the Cold War had played a significant role in the confrontation and conflicts in South Asia between India and Pakistan, but the Cold War was not the root cause of them, and they continued after its end. Pakistani opposition to India's position in divided Kashmir was a key cause of tension, as the Pakistani government supported Muslim insurgents, while also using this issue in order to bolster domestic support for both government and military. The Pakistani government was encouraged by the success of its Taliban allies in Afghanistan, and this led it to press India over Kashmir. The extent to which insurgency operations could lead to fighting between regular forces was shown in 1999 when the Pakistani military, having moved its troops onto the Indian side of the Line of Control, disguised them as local guer-rillas.

The subsequent Kargil conflict, which was won by India, reflected the value of determination and firepower at the tactical level, combined action at the operational, and political will and skill at the strategic. In the first, there was a willingness on the part of the Indians not only to attack in the face of well-defended positions but also to use artillery to destroy these positions. As so often with the warfare of the period covered by this book, it is a serious mistake to underrate the potential and use of artillery, not least by underplaying it in contrast to air power. In operational terms, air power played a valuable role in the Kargil conflict, not least by hitting Pakistani logistics. At the strategic level, a well-conceived but also limited Indian plan, for clearing the Indian zone but not escalating the conflict by crossing the Line of Con-trol, helped maintain domestic support and win that of the USA, and without enabling the defeated Pakistani military to stoke up backs-to-the-wall domestic support.[2]

At a very different level of scale, there was also continuity in tension within states such as the sectarian riots in the Ferghana Valley in Uzbekistan in 1988 which became more serious once the Cold War came to an end (see p. 26). As another instance of a conflict that, like those in Angola and El Salvador, was part of the Cold War but not defined by it, there was a long-standing civil war in Sudan which had been waged from 1963 until 1972, and then again from 1983. Successive governments based in the Arabic-speaking Muslim north thwarted southern separatism but were unable to subjugate the vast region. The southern sepa-ratists of the Anya-Nya movement had initially lacked modern weapons, many relying on spears, but their use of guerrilla tactics gravely weakened the Sudanese army's position in the south. The size of Sudan also told against the army, which, on the other hand, was more successful in its policy of turning for support to the Nuer tribe, rivals of the Dinka tribe, which was prominent in the resistance. The latter, however, increasingly benefited from inter-national support. Thus, the ground-to-air missiles of the Sudan

People's Liberation Army made the aerial resupply of government garrisons hazardous, while the attack on the government's oil pipeline at Atbara in 1999 demonstrated the state's vulnerability.

Ethnic and regional issues were not only intertwined in Sudan. For example, at a smaller scale, they were seen in a conflict in the Caprivi Strip of Namibia that began to receive international attention in 1999. Like many Third World conflicts, one side sought to overturn imperial territorial settlements, and the warfare reflected the failure of the state to incorporate minorities. In the former case, a secession attempt was mounted by the Lozi-speaking people of Caprivi, who are dominated by the Ovambo majority of Namibia. In 1999, about 200 fighters of the Caprivi Liberation Army attacked key points in the provincial capital, Katima Mulilo, but the ill-planned attack was swiftly defeated. Paramilitaries from the Special Field Force and members of the Central Intelligence Service then seized large numbers of suspects and treated them brutally.

This is a small-scale conflict which was widely ignored and can be readily omitted from books in which space is at a premium, but it is instructive for throwing light on a type and degree of tension and violence that is widespread around much of the world. In considering ethnicity, however, it is necessary to note the extent to which it involves elements of construction, with cultural and political beliefs and practices serving to entrench differences and a sense of ethnic consciousness. Conflict and the recollection of conflict can play a major role in this process.

At a different level of scale to the Caprivi Strip, Indonesia, a successful non-Western imperial power, had successfully annexed western New Guinea (as West Irian) from the Dutch in 1963 and East Timor as the Portuguese empire collapsed in 1975. Demands for independence, by the Free Papua Movement in Irian and the Fretilin (Frente Revolucionária de Timor-Leste Independente; Revolutionary Front for an Independent East Timor) movement in East Timor, were brutally resisted. The reliance on force in East Timor proved seriously counterproductive, as it failed to assuage local separatism and also led to international condemnation, especially after the shooting of unarmed demonstrators at a cemetery in Dili on 12 November 1991 led to hundreds of deaths or injuries and was filmed by Western journalists.

In 1999, the Indonesians responded to continued separatism and to international pressure by giving East Timor the choice of independence or regional autonomy. The people overwhelmingly chose independence, despite serious pressure from militias supported by the army. After the election, the coercion was stepped up, but international attention and anger mounted and finally led the Indonesians to accept the popular verdict. Australian forces under UN auspices secured the new situation, while in Indonesia failure helped discredit the government. Bin Laden chose to see East Timor's independence as a blow to the Muslim world (Indonesia is preponderantly Muslim) and first criticised Australia as a result of its intervention there.

The Indonesian government was more successful in resisting separatism in western New Guinea and in Aceh in Sumatra. In part, this reflected the lack of international attention and intervention, but there was also a stronger drive for independence in East Timor, which had been a Portuguese, rather than (like the rest of Indonesia) Dutch, colony prior to Indonesian control.

Separatism was not the sole cause of conflict across the Indonesian archipelago. More generally, the 1990s brought a strengthening of ethnic tension and regional consciousness, with widespread violence. Thus, in Kalimantan (Indonesian Borneo), from 1997, native Dayaks fought Madurans who had immigrated since the 1950s, in part with government encouragement: thinking of Indonesia as a unit, the government sought to move people from areas of overcrowding without the consent of the population in the receiving area. Beheading played a major role in the violence: it was important in traditional Dayak culture as it was seen as the way to win favourable magic. Similarly, in Assam in north-east India, the separatist United Liberation Front of Asom directed much of its violence against migrant workers from elsewhere in India, for example in 2007.

The numbers involved in conflict between Third World states and opposing movements could be considerable. In 1999, it was estimated that Indian security forces resisting insurgency in Kashmir, forces which included not only the army but also the Central

Reserve Police Force and the Border Security Force, numbered 400,000. As an instance of the potential scale of conventional conflict in the Third World, in 2000 Ethiopia invaded Eritrea during a war that had broken out in 1998 and was a frontier struggle that was also a conflict over hegemony. As with many Third World conflicts, it is difficult to be precise about numbers and events, but the Ethiopians benefited from superior air power, better armour (Russian T-72 tanks) and greater numbers, only to find that the Eritreans fought well, taking advantage of the terrain. A settlement was arranged by the UN that year, but not before about a fifth of the Eritrean population had been displaced.

In contrast, in Liberia from 1989 and Sierra Leone from 1991, the chaos that accompanied what was referred to as 'failed states' saw conflict that lacked much central direction. In both, drugged teenagers (many of them orphans) and outright looters had little, if any, idea of the cause they were fighting for, except for their own personal gain. The use of child soldiers, also seen with insurrectionary movements in Nepal and Uganda, can be regarded as an aspect of the totality of these struggles, although, looked at differently, this use was also a reflection of the extent to which Western norms were not followed. Political objectives, beyond the capture of power, were hazy, and 'wars' benefited from the large-scale availability of small arms and were financed primarily by criminal operations and forced extortions. There were no chains of command or (often) even uniforms that distinguished 'troops' from each other, or from other fighters, and, politically, this was an instance of a more widespread process in which warlords moved from being rebels to presidents or vice versa, while ethnicity helped exacerbate conflict.[3]

In response, the Nigerian army played a role in peacekeeping in Sierra Leone and Liberia, although this also reflected its own regional agenda. Poorly trained for the task, the Nigerians tended to use firepower as a substitute for policing, although, in both cases, the situation was very difficult: drug-taking adolescent fighters operating on behalf of factions had reduced both countries to a form of gangland chaos, and this made it difficult for regulars to identify opponents who could be defeated. In Sierra Leone, where a private military company, Executive Outcomes, had proved a crucial support to the government, the civil war was declared over in January 2002, and an international peacekeeping force began to disarm combatants. In Liberia, a coup in 1980 was followed by a rebellion by Charles Taylor started in 1989. He became President in 1997, but a rebellion against him, which began in 1999, led to his opponents advancing into the capital, Monrovia, in 2003. Taylor resigned in the subsequent chaos, and Nigerian peacekeepers took over Monrovia.

In Rwanda, in Central Africa, civil war was not so disorganised, but it was even more bloody. In 1990, the Tutsi émigrés of the Rwanda Patriot Front invaded Rwanda from Uganda. There, in an example of the interrelationship of struggles in different states, the Tutsi Rwandan Patriotic Front (RPF) and its army, the Rwanda Patriotic Army (RPA), fought with Ugandans under Yoweri Museveni against the dictators Idi Amin and Milton Obote, deposing Obote in 1985. After Museveni won, the RPA had his support when they invaded Rwanda in 1990. The initial invasion failed and led to the RPF taking shelter in the mountainous Virunga region. In 1991, a more wide-ranging offensive by the well-led RPF kept the initiative away from the government forces. By 1993, the capital, Kigali, was under threat by the RPF. As a result, the government was willing to accept a peace agreement in August 1993 which was monitored by a small, largely Belgian, UN peacekeeping force.

In 1993, however, a Tutsi coup in neighbouring Burundi against the Hutu government led to the killing of over 100,000 Hutus, increasing tension in Rwanda. In April the following year, an extremist group of Hutus seized power in Rwanda, touching off the slaughter of about 937,000 Tutsi and moderate Hutus: the figure may have been over 1 million, one in seven of the population. Rather than seeing the violence simply in terms of ethnic division, each ethnic group was divided between moderates and extremists.

The failure of the international community to prevent genocide, not least to send reinforcements or instructions to the UN Assistance Mission for Rwanda, raised a question mark against both the UN's ability to enforce norms and the willingness of the world's leading power, the USA, to act. France itself was partly responsible for the crisis. Drawing on a long-standing tradition, which President Mitterrand had expressed while a minister in the 1950s, the French government saw an Anglo-Saxon threat to *Françafrique,* a zone including not only former French but also the ex-Belgian colonies of Rwanda, Burundi and Congo. Regarding the RPA as an Anglo-Saxon-backed Ugandan army, the French government had dispatched troops to help the Hutu regime in the civil war of 1990–3. Large amounts of arms, moreover, were sent to the Rwandan army, which was put under effective French control. The French proved willing to encourage the Hutu extremists to slaughter the Tutsis, including direct assistance in the genocide launched in April 1994, as well as in earlier killings.

After the Hutu regime was overthrown in July 1994 by the ably commanded and well-disciplined RPA, the French government sent its military to assist its Hutu allies in taking refuge in camps at Goma in Congo, where the presence of the Hutus helped accelerate the crisis in Congo. Yet again, it proved impossible to isolate conflict, and Rwandan and Ugandan forces intervened against the Hutus in Congo from November 1996. Rwanda claimed that President Mobutu Sese Soko, the dictator of Congo, a long-term ally of France, was not restraining the Hutu extremists in Congo. Initially, the Rwanda forces had operated only against the Hutu camps, but the reinforcement of the Hutu *genocidaires* by Mobutu and their movement into the interior led the RPA, in turn, to advance. Mobutu's demoralised army disintegrated as they did so. RPA forces walked to Kinshasa, the Congolese capital, and to the Atlantic, a distance of over 2,000 kilometres. This advance led to the overthrow of the Mobutu government in May 1997, again much to the irritation of the French government.[4]

Laurent Kabila, the corrupt President of Congo, who replaced Mobutu, turned, however, against his recent Rwandan and Ugandan allies, leading to a new war in 1998, with Rwandan units again attacking eastern Congo. They had less success when they tried to capture Kinshasa, being beaten by more strongly armed forces from Angola and Zimbabwe which had intervened in support of Kabila. The war continued until 2002. Yet further confusing the situation, and indicating the range of competing interests, Rwandan and Ugandan forces themselves clashed in 1999–2000 (see also pp. 91–2).

State borders inherited from old imperial boundaries that cut across perceived ethnic and tribal configurations contributed significantly to such interventions. This interventionism also reflected an overlap between international and domestic conflict. In some cases, this overlap can be seen as an aspect of warfare, in others of large-scale feuding, and in some of politics. Disputes between local peoples and states had often interacted with, first, the spread of Western imperialism and, subsequently, the Cold War, as the protagonists in the latter sought local allies. This pattern continued after the Cold War ended, with parties to disputes seeking powerful outside supporters that could offer international backing and provide arms.

In Burundi, the civil war which started in 1993 continued into the 2000s despite efforts to stop it. Over 150,000 people were killed, and at least three quarters of a million became refugees. The Tutsi-dominated army there was opposed by Hutu militia. Ethnic violence was also common elsewhere in Africa, for example in Mauritania, where clashes between Africans and Arabs (blacks and Moors) led to violence in 1989–90, and Nigeria where, it has been claimed, over 50,000 people were killed between 2001 and 2004. Such conflicts were a modern demonstration of the argument that a general tendency of 'primitive' warfare is to cause higher casualty rates than the majority of conflicts involving regular forces.[5] The number of combatants in such 'primitive' warfare is also higher as it is not restricted to regular forces. In turn, the greater number of casualties reflects the anti-societal character of much of such warfare, a character summed up in the term 'ethnic cleansing'.

At a very different scale, force was also displayed as an integral part of the political process, although any listing has to note the very different levels of violence seen in coups, which, in large part, reflected their contrasting causes. Coups were an important part of the military history of the period. The politicisation of the military by civilian governments keen to use its strength to help achieve their goals also helped encourage the military to overcome inhibitions to the use of force.[6] Other coups were the product of intermilitary divisions. Coups in Africa included those in Mali (1991), the highly unstable Comoros archipelago in the Pacific (1995 and 1999), in Niger (1996 and 1999), Sierra Leone (1997), Ivory Coast (1999), Mauritania (2005 and 2008) and Togo (2005).

Coups reflected both the ambitions of the military and also the willingness to turn to foreign support. Thus, in Congo-Brazzaville, Denis Sassou Nguesso, an army officer active in coups and coup attempts in the 1960s and 1970s, and President from 1979, did not accept his loss of power in the elections of 1992 and, instead, turned to civil war, drawing on support from French oil interests, which were, and are, closely linked to the French government, and on militias from Congo. He finally regained power in 1997. In Asia, a military regime was created in Pakistan in 1999.

Coups in Latin America occurred in Haiti in 1991 and 2004, and in Ecuador in 2000. The use of force both played a role in changes in civilian government, such as those in Peru and Colombia in the 1980s and 1990s, and also led to the creation of military governments, reflecting the widespread conviction among Latin American militaries that their function included the suppression of internal enemies. In 1992, the Peruvian president, Alberto Fujimori, used the army to shut down Congress and the courts.

Control over the military was even more important to the Castro regime in Cuba. A key player, Fidel Castro's brother, Raúl, was First Vice-President and Defence Minister. The latter controlled the 50,000 regulars of the FAR (Fuerzas Armadas Revolucionarias; Cuban Revolutionary Armed Forces), as well as the million-plus reservists and territorial militia. In 1989, the Ministry of the Interior was subordinated to the FAR, which gave Raúl Castro authority over the 15,000 police.

Some military regimes were short term, such as that created in Niger in 1999, when the President was shot dead by the head of his bodyguard, who then seized power. More impressively, Colonel Ely Vall, the head of the secret service, who seized power in Mauritania in 2005 in a bloodless coup, overthrowing Maaouya Taya, President from 1984, promised elections within two years in which no coup leader would compete. Free elections were indeed held in 2007, but a fresh coup occurred in 2008.

Other military regimes, in contrast, were long-lasting. In Myanmar (Burma), where the military ruled as the State Peace and Development Council, the elections held in 1990 were annulled when a pro-democracy movement won, and the military has held onto power since. In Nigeria, after a coup on 31 December 1983, rule by the Supreme Military Council (1984–5) saw the use of troops to suppress strikes and demonstrations. This corrupt regime was followed by a coup in August 1985 by the Chief of Staff, General Ibrahim Babangida. Losing the presidential election in June 1993 to Moshood Abiola, who was not from the military, he annulled the election, but the ensuing instability and violence led Babangida to hand over power to an Interim Governing Council (IGC) led by his ally Ernest Shonekan. In turn, the IGC was overthrown that November in a coup by General Sani Abacha, the Minister of Defence, who declared himself Commander-in-Chief and Head of State.

As with many coups, this was as much a coup against other groups in the military as against civil society. Babangida's allies in the military were forcibly retired, while Abiola was imprisoned until his death in 1998. The military joined the police in violently suppressing opposition activities including demonstrations. Force was also used to suppress the Ogoni of the oil-rich Niger delta who demanded autonomy. Abacha remained dictator until he died of a heart attack in June 1998. Another general, Abdulsalami Abubakar, came to power as a result of action by his colleagues, but he decided on democracy, and free elections were held in 1999.

In the short term, authoritarian regimes reliant on force were less powerful or rigid in practice than they appeared, and they operated by accepting the circumvention of their nostrums and structures by their own members, as well as by vested interests and by the public itself. In the long term, these regimes found it difficult to contain political problems and to satisfy popular demands. Thus, the military lost power in Bangladesh and Chile in 1990, the first as a result of popular demonstrations, and in Thailand in 1992, while in Indonesia, General Suharto, the army chief of staff, who had taken over power in 1967, was forced to surrender power in 1998: he had been discredited as corrupt and was put under considerable political and popular pressure. The TNI (Tentera Nasional Indonesia; Indonesian National Military), however, remained important in Indonesian politics and, far more, to the Indonesian state.[7] The Thai army staged another coup in 2006, although it swiftly accepted a return to democracy.

At the same time, the major role of the military in the economy increased its impact in many states, for example in Indonesia and Pakistan. Aside from economic distortions, distortions which the military concealed, and the major effect on public finances, this role also influenced the political process. The impact of the military in this fashion indicated the extent to which they could serve as a costly protection system that constrained the possibilities for government. The subsidies their uneconomic companies received were as pernicious as unnecessary procurement policies.[8]

Unsuccessful coups, and indeed plans for coups, were also an important and instructive aspect of military history. Failed coups included those in Mauritania and Nigeria in 1990, Russia in 1991, Equatorial Guinea in 1997 and 2004, and Congo in 2004. The significance of attempted coups helped ensure that governments had to see coup avoidance and suppression as one of the most important tasks of their military policy. Careful attempts were made to woo the military and, at the same time, to lessen its power by building up rival paramilitary services. The attempt to create links with the military led rulers to foster personal and symbolic relations, with Hafez al-Assad, the President of Syria, having his son and intended successor join the army in 1994: he became President in 2000. Rival paramilitary services were important in a number of states, for example Saudi Arabia, Iraq and Yemen, leading to the counterpointing of the army with the National Guard in Saudi Arabia, the Central Security Forces in Egypt, the Defence Regiments in Syria and the Republican Guard in Iraq and Iran. A stress on coup avoidance represents a way to approach military history which is totally different to the established one.

CHAPTER 4

THE WAR ON TERROR

Writing about a period that is in progress poses many problems, not least those of significance and sympathy. More particularly, the future becomes present and can readily upset the analysis. Will the American-led clash with radical Muslim fundamentalism, for example, be any more than an interlude before great-power confrontation revives and poses new challenges for the American military?

The surprise attacks launched by Osama Bin Laden's al-Qaeda terrorist movement on New York and Washington on 11 September 2001 led to about 3,220 fatalities, the majority in the Twin Towers in New York.[1] This terrorist employment of Weapons of Mass Effect transformed American attitudes, focused American concerns and ensured that the American government took a more determined position in warfare in the early 2000s than had been the case in the Balkans in the late 1990s. The replacement of Bill Clinton by George W. Bush as President in early 2001 was also significant, in that Bush was more prone to adopt a militarised response; while, at least initially after 11 September, the Americans benefited from widespread international support in their self-proclaimed 'War on Terrorism'. Concerned to 'dry up the swamp', the American government found it essential, in resisting terrorism, and in particular the challenge posed by suicide terrorism, to strike back and to be seen to regain the initiative. This response led to attacks, overt and covert, on what were identified as terrorist bases and supporters, attacks which represented another stage in the movement towards action that had followed the end of the Cold War. There was parallel action against terrorist financial networks.

Before plunging on with the narrative of American action, and the consideration of how far it matched notions of an RMA, it is pertinent to offer a context by considering how far other attempted 'revolutions in military affairs' require discussion, in particular those sought by terrorist groups and by so-called rogue states. In the first case, the attempt in 2001 by al-Qaeda to use terrorist methods to a strategic end by crippling, or at least symbolically dethroning, American financial and political power failed, not least because it rested on a greatly flawed assumption about the concentrated and top-down nature of American power. There was also a misplaced assumption that it would prove possible to crack American morale, although it has been argued that al-Qaeda was surprised by the impact of its attack.

Nevertheless, the attack also indicated the extent to which the terrorist repertoire was far from fixed. Although it is true that al-Qaeda did not deploy weapons of mass destruction in 2001, its ability to make use of Western technology, in this case civilian aircraft, like the determination it shared with many other terrorist movements, to ignore any boundaries between military and civilian, indicated the challenge it posed. Similarly, in March 2004, the Western dependence on public transport was exploited in the al-Qaeda attacks on commuter trains in Madrid.

Al-Qaeda's apocalyptic and millenarian aspirations and tendencies also make it particularly serious as it is difficult to see how the threat it poses can be lessened through negotiation. Moreover, the extent to which, like Nazism, al-Qaeda appears in part to function by supporters seeking to work towards the leader's declared aspirations increases its deadliness, as dislocating the structure of the formal organisation will not therefore end the threat. This point underlines the extent to which there is a cultural challenge rather than one from a network that can be defeated by such conventional means as destroying the leadership.

This terrorism is a more serious problem for international relations than those posed by particular aggressive states because the nature of a stateless entity is that it does not need to respond to the constraints that arise from claims to sovereign power, although such stateless groups are also in a competition for legitimacy. The military equivalent to the lack of constraints is that these stateless entities may not have a territorial space that can be attacked or occupied. As a result of this lack of constraint, the challenge posed by terrorist movements can seem greater than that from terrorist states, especially as the movements can seek to base themselves in 'failed states', such as Afghanistan and Somalia, where it is difficult to take action short of full-scale military intervention against them. Moreover, these movements can take place in war by proxy, such as Iran's use of Hizbullah. Although most terrorism is in fact aimed at states in the Third World, where the number of victims is also far higher (a large number of them are Muslims), the challenge from terrorism is particularly notable for strong powers, especially the strongest, the USA, as they have less practicable need to fear attack from other states than weaker states do: were the forces of these states to attack the USA, they would be defeated, and their territory could certainly be attacked.

This distinction, however, is challenged by the attempt by rogue states to acquire weapons of mass destruction and related delivery systems. In the early 1990s, it was discovered that North Korea was developing plutonium, which could be used to make nuclear warheads, and in 2002 it admitted to be trying to enrich uranium. In 1998, moreover, North Korea tested a medium-range Taepodong missile, firing it over Japan into the Pacific. North Korea was not alone: concern over Iran's nuclear ambitions became more pronounced in the mid-2000s.

The overthrow of the Saddam regime in Iraq in 2003 encouraged the governments of North Korea and Iran to press ahead with such schemes as they thought the presence of weapons of mass destruction likely to deter American attack. Although the regular forces of states such as North Korea and Iran probably lack the capability and ability in defence to defeat the conventional forces of stronger powers, and certainly could not stage an effective offensive war, such weapons of mass destruction would enable them to threaten these forces and, perhaps even eventually, home territory, while the real or potential availability of such weapons would also challenge the aspect of international aspirations and force projection represented by interventionist policies and alliance systems.

The challenge from terrorism appeared to mark a key stage in the ending of the Cold War. In 2001, Russia lent diplomatic support to the American air offensive against the Taliban regime in Afghanistan, which had provided sanctuary for al-Qaeda. This support was despite the fact that this American campaign, launched on 7 October, entailed the establishment of American bases in Central Asian republics that had until 1991 been part of the Soviet Union, such as Uzbekistan, and Russia was particularly sensitive to the establishment of bases in former parts of the Soviet Union.

The Taliban had emerged from the chaos that was Afghanistan in the early 1990s. The Afghan regime of President Mohammad Najibullah, who had been put in power by the Soviets in 1986, finally fell in April 1992 when the guerrillas entered the capital, Kabul: the government had been greatly weakened by the defection of its northern strongman, Abdul Rashid Dostum. Victory, however, for the guerrillas was followed by an upsurge in already strong ethnic regional tensions within Afghanistan. In particular, the northerners, who had seized the capital in 1992, were opposed by Gulbuddin Hekmatyar, a Pushtun and the leader of the Afghanistan Islamic Party, who attacked Kabul. As the country was divided by warlords and the economy collapsed, feeding the flight of refugees, looting became the best way to supply warring forces.

This situation was challenged by the Kandahar-based and Pakistan-backed Taliban movement, which sought control over the entire country and wanted to impose a fervent religious orthodoxy. Benefiting from Pushtun support (the Pushtuns span the frontier between Afghanistan and Pakistan), as well as from the ample profits of opium-dealing, and from a strong conviction of divine mission, the Taliban overran much of the country in 1996, seizing Kabul that year. Pakistan provided help because victory for a Pushtun protégé movement was seen as a way to limit Indian regional influence and to give Pakistan strategic depth in any conflict with India. Indeed, this policy provided a key instance of the degree to which the 'War on Terror' was mediated through pre-existing rivalries and geopolitical structures. This process was scarcely new, but it helped explain the problems faced by the USA in dealing with its allies.[2]

Bribes helped dissolve much of the opposition to the Taliban, but, in the non-Pushtun areas, particularly in the north, the Taliban encountered serious resistance, which stopped its advance. Moreover, this resistance helped provide the Americans with allies when they attacked the Taliban regime in 2001, in the aftermath of the 11 September attacks on New York and Washington. The Taliban, in practice, had little to offer in Afghanistan bar ceaseless struggle against heretics and infidels, and this was central to its brutality towards those with whom it disagreed.

The Taliban regime refused to hand over Osama Bin Laden and other al-Qaeda members for trial, seeing them, instead, as defenders of Islam. Mistakenly confident as a result of the failure of Soviet occupation in the 1980s, the Taliban did not appreciate that the Americans posed a more formidable threat. As a result of the failure to hand over al-Qaeda leaders, Afghanistan became the target for American action, and with the full support of the UN.

This action was rapidly effective, with American Special Forces teams infiltrated from 19 October 2001. They played a key role in calling down and guiding large-scale American close air support. Taliban forces in the north were heavily battered. The regime's fall indeed was seen as a success for American air power, which included long-range B-52 and B-1 'stealth' bombers, extensive aerial refueling – enabling planes to fly very long missions, Tomahawk Cruise missiles from warships in the Arabian Sea, AC-130 gunships, unpiloted drones providing reconnaissance or firing missiles and CBU-130 'Combined-Effects Munitions' which spread cluster bombs. The availability of dual mode, laser and GPS (Global Positioning Systems) guidance for bombs increased the range of precision available, while the air assault benefited from the effective and, crucially, rapid management of information from a number of sources, including forward air controllers and ground-based GPS devices. In addition, the absence of hostile air power and of effective anti-aircraft fire was important.

The Taliban, however, ultimately had to be overcome on the ground by rival Afghan forces, particularly the United Front, the so-called Northern Alliance. In doing so, the lack of coherence of the Taliban regime, and the porosity and changeable nature of alignments in Afghanistan, were both important to the war's outcome and far more so than air-power enthusiasts were to accept. Warlords switched allegiance, in large part as a result of bribes, and the Taliban position collapsed on 9–13 November 2001 with the fall of the cities of Mazar-e Sharif, Herat and Kabul. The Taliban was unable to regroup after the fall of Mazar-e Sharif, not least because defections that stemmed from its divisions accentuated a failure of command and control. American air power and Afghan ground attack combined to ensure the fall of the more firmly defended city of Kunduz on 23 November. Taliban forces tried to regroup at Kandahar, but, as their regime unravelled, abandoned it on 7 December.

The Taliban position had been broken by the combination of American and Afghan assault, the latter an instance of the proxy warfare seen throughout the Cold War, while the willingness, under heavy American pressure, of President Pervez Musharraf of neighbouring Pakistan to cut, at least ostensibly, links with the Taliban and to provide assistance, including permitting American over-flying and moving Pakistani troops into border areas, was important. The American air attack helped switch the local political balance within Afghanistan.[3] Some of the fighting was traditional, with Northern Alliance forces using cavalry charges. At the same time, for example on 9 November on the approach to Mazar-e Sharif from the south, B-52s were needed to overcome Taliban defences which included multiple rocket launchers.

Nevertheless, the victorious campaign did not lead to the clear-cut pro-American triumph that had been hoped for. Instead, it became readily apparent that the war had provoked a regrouping and realignment of factions, uneasily presided over by the weak, new pro-Western President, Hamid Karzai, whose power extended little further than the capital, Kabul. This range was far better than nothing, but it did not amount to forcing opponents to accept the will of the victor, let alone the legitimacy of this government.

Furthermore, analysis of the impact of the air attack revealed that, while it had been considerable in the initial attacks in northern Afghanistan, it subsequently became less so in the ground operations launched by Afghanistan and allied forces against Taliban and al-Qaeda survivors in Tora Bora (December 2001) and in

Operation Anaconda, south of Gardiz (March 2002). This decline in effectiveness, which underlined the already-known limitations of air power for suppressing insurgents,[4] was attributed to the Taliban ability to respond by taking advantage of extremely difficult terrain features, for camouflage and cover.[5] In the absence of adequate air cover during stages of Operation Anaconda, Taliban mortars inflicted damage.[6] In that operation, helicopters provided important fire support and lift for the Afghan forces, but also they took damage from ground fire to which they are very vulnerable. Al-Qaeda and the Taliban stood and fought, thwarting the initial American-led Afghan ground attack. Eventually, however, al-Qaeda and Taliban forces were overcome after more Afghan and American support was provided.

More generally, there was also the key problem posed by a reliance on local allies who, understandably, had their own agenda, a problem that has affected alliances and imperial powers across the centuries. The Americans had found the Northern Alliance a beneficial partner, but that was because their goals were shared. This situation no longer proved the case in operations in Tora Bora, and the lack of effective American ground forces to act as a substitute proved crucial. This lack may have helped Bin Laden to escape, and he has not been captured since. The failure to capture Bin Laden represents a major failure as, whatever his particular command significance, especially now, this failure led to a sense of impotence. Moreover, Pakistani support for the Taliban, especially from the influential ISS, helped Taliban and al-Qaeda forces to retreat into Pakistan from Tora Bora.

The problem of partnership between the USA and local allies was to recur in the American aftermath of the invasion of Iraq in 2003, with the assumption that the tempo of local politics could be directed to produce political cooperation as well as allied forces willing to act on American terms again proving mistaken. Indeed, a careful reading of the Afghan conflict, not least of the aftermath to the collapse of the Taliban regime, should have encouraged greater caution in planning for Iraq. There are few signs, however, that such a reading affected the decision-makers, in part because wish-fulfilment played a key role in their attitudes and ambience.

Operations by the International Security Assistance Force against al-Qaeda supporters in Afghanistan were the most prominent aspect of the American and American-allied War on Terror that followed the attacks of 11 September 2001. Not only Americans and Afghans were involved. Thus, the British government proved eager to send not only special forces but also ground forces into Afghanistan. The latter took over the key air base at Bagram near Kabul in November 2001 as a move intended to help nation-building.

Operations in Afghanistan were far from the only moves prior to the Iraq invasion. Instead, American special operations units were deployed against Muslim terrorist movements linked to al-Qaeda. This process was particularly so on and near the Philippine island of Mindanao where, from 2003, the Americans provided military support to the army against the Abu Sayyaf group in a long-standing confrontation that came near to settlement in 2008. Also in 2003, the pro-Western republic of Georgia was provided with help against an al-Qaeda force in the region of the Pankisi Gorge, which was also a base for Chechen rebels.

Terrorism linked to al-Qaeda affected a number of countries. Thus, to take the Muslim world, Turkey was hit by suicide bombings in 2003, Saudi Arabia in 2003–4, Jordan in 2005 and Algiers in 2007. Terrorist links were not always easy to unravel. The suicide bombers who, in March 2004, struck Tashkent, the capital of Uzbekistan, then an American ally, and also a Muslim state, may have been linked to al-Qaeda via the Islamic Movement of Uzbekistan, members of whom served as jihadists in Afghanistan and Pakistan. Abortive terrorist attacks included those in Singapore in 2001 and Jordan in 2004.

There was an (understandable) tendency to treat all militant Islamic groups as closely linked even though the key element was often as much indigenous causes. Thus, Algerian terrorists were linked to al-Qaeda, with which they formally merged in 2006, but the root cause of the violence by Muslim militants within Algeria was the decision in 1992 by the State Council to ban the Islamic Salvation Front and to proclaim a state of emergency, a measure taken in order to preserve power in the face of the electoral appeal of the Front. This action led to a civil war which remained at a high level until 1999 and which resulted in over 100,000 deaths and, maybe, over 150,000. In turn, this conflict helped make violence normative in Algeria, and it has also become a base for terrorist attacks elsewhere, a process helped by the Algerian diaspora, both in France and Britain.

Al-Qaeda was keen to assert links between such struggles, as they were seen as ways to aid recruitment and fund-raising: al-Qaeda portrays Islam as under consistent attack from without and within, an attack requiring a violent defence. Yet, the links, for example with the militants responsible for suicide bombers in Morocco in 2003 and 2007, could be tenuous. Furthermore, there were rivalries within the fundamentalist camp, for example between Waziris and Uzbeks in Pakistan in 2007. Indeed, the Waziris were able to draw on support from the army in this fighting. These rivalries were part of a more general process in which local fundamentalists often resent foreign jihadists. This tension is a reflection of the multiple differences within Islam, the strong sense of ethnic distinction, competition over resources and disagreements over leadership and tactics. All are underplayed by broad-brush talk of the War on Terror.

For states confronting terrorism, counter-terrorist operations posed serious difficulties, not least the identification of opponents and the brevity of the period in which it is possible to engage with them, problems which were greatly exacerbated by the terrorists' use of suicide as a method. Under the guise of 'martyrdom', this indeed is al-Qaeda's trademark, one designed to cause massive casualties.

There are also conceptual problems in such conflict which are linked to the question of policy. The terminology used towards opponents delegitimises them: instead of 'freedom fighters' and 'war', we have 'terrorists' and 'terrorism', but this terminology can make it more difficult to conceive of a strategy that matches political with military methods and goals. As a result, this approach may make it harder to probe the possibilities for an exit strategy. On the other hand, the extreme anti-Western position and millenarian goals of al-Qaeda and its allies, and its apparent relish for extraordinary violence, do not make negotiations an option.

Aside from the specific need to respond to al-Qaeda, not least to lessen the chance of fresh attacks, it is not surprising, in light of its strategic culture and governmental assumptions, that the USA sought a military solution for what appeared to be its more general strategic crisis. The National Security Strategy issued in September 2002 was strategically and operationally ambitious. Pressing the need for pre-emptive strikes, in response to what were seen as the dual threats of terrorist regimes and 'rogue states' possessing or developing weapons of mass destruction, the strategy sought to transform the global political order to lessen the chance of these threats developing. To that end, the first paragraph proposed a universalist message that linked the end of the Cold War to the new challenge:

The great struggles of the twentieth century between liberty and totalitarianism ended with a decisive victory for the forces of freedom [. . .] These values of freedom are right and true for every person, in every society – and the duty of these values against their enemies is the common calling of freedom-loving people across the globe and across the ages [. . .] We will extend the peace by encouraging free and open societies on every continent.

In an interesting echo, General Yuri Baluevsky, the Chief of the Russian General Staff, declared on 8 September 2004 that Russia could deliver pre-emptive strikes on terrorist bases anywhere in the world. In the hands of some excitable writers, the notion of preemption was pushed very far indeed. John Keegan wrote:

The World Trade Centre outrage was coordinated on the internet [. . .] If Washington is serious in its determination to eliminate terrorism, it will have to forbid internet providers to allow the transmission of encrypted messages [. . .] Uncompliant providers on foreign territory should expect their buildings to be destroyed by cruise missiles.[7]

Striking against terrorist bases, as in Afghanistan, became part of an American doctrine, named the Bush Doctrine, of pre-

emptive attack against hostile states. As a result, conflict returned
to the Persian Gulf in early 2003 when Iraq was attacked by a preponderantly American force, with the participation of a large sec-
tion of the British military and of small Australian, Polish, Czech
and Slovak contingents. However, the coalition involved was far
smaller than that in 1991, not least with the absence of Arab and
French participation. Moreover, King Abdullah would not allow
the USA to advance into Iraq from Saudi Arabia, and Turkey also
refused transit, a key development as such consent had initially
been anticipated.

The campaign, and the preparations for it, were conducted in
the glare of media attention and pundit discussion, and there was
considerable speculation as to how far it corresponded with current
notions about an RMA as well as related debates about the character of modern Western military capability and development. Iraq
provided the USA with a definite (and defiant) target with regular
armed forces rather than the more intangible struggle with terrorism, which challenged Western conventions of war-making. The
attack was presented in terms of 'drying up the swamp' – elimi-
nating a state allegedly supporting terrorism, for example against
Israel (although not in fact, despite claims, backing al-Qaeda), as
well, more specifically, as destroying Iraq's supposed capability in
weapons of mass destruction and ending Iraq's breaching of UN
resolutions. There were particular concerns about Iraqi chemical
and bacteriological warheads, and, indeed, the conviction that
they existed affected the military planning and also encouraged
an early attack. Although the claims about Iraqi weapons of mass
destruction were subsequently to be discredited, it is clear that
Iraqi ministers believed that they had such weapons.

Operation Iraqi Freedom, the American-led and dominated
campaign in Iraq in 2003, with its rapid and successful advance
up the Euphrates valley on Baghdad, was widely praised for its
manoeuvrist character and for its ability to gain and seize the initiative, disorientating the Iraqi military and government and hitting
their capacity to respond. The key elements were the 125,000 US
combat troops on the ground, although Britain supplied 45,000
troops and Australia 2,000. Predictions that the Iraqis would use
chemical weapons and blow up bridges and dams, or that it would

be hard to overrun the Iraqi cities and that they would pose problems like those faced by the Germans in Stalingrad in 1942, with the American military being chewed up in the course of their capture, were totally disproved.

These predictions had rested on the assumption that the Iraqis had responded to their defeat in 1991 by deciding not to contest the Americans in manoeuvrist warfare (the technology of which would give the Americans an advantage) and, instead, to abandon the desert and focus on the cities, hoping to repeat the success of Mohamed Aidid in Mogadishu in 1993 (see pp. 21–2). Indeed, both in 1991 and in 2003, Saddam Hussein appears to have counted on the Americans suffering if they could be forced to abandon the distant use of firepower for close combat. He appears to have anticipated that the problems of urban warfare would lessen American technological advantages and lead to casualties that obliged the American government to change policy.[8]

If so, Saddam's analysis was certainly mistaken in the short term and, anyway, could not prevent conquest by a well-organised and high-tempo American-dominated invasion force. This conquest was a result that suggested that America's opponents elsewhere would need to turn to other methods of deterrence and opposition, most obviously nuclear arms. The coherence of the Iraqi regime, its ability to intimidate the population and the possibility of exploiting American vulnerability along their long lines of advance were all hit by the high tempo of American attacks and the ability to sustain the advance at this rate. This tempo accentuated weaknesses in the regime, including its long-standing fear of the Iraqi military and concern about the possibility of coups. The Iraqi attacks on American supply lines, for example at the Euphrates bridge town of Nasiriya, attracted considerable media attention, but the forces available for such attacks were a local irritant that could be bypassed on the drive on Baghdad rather than operationally significant. Despite short-term problems, which were understandable given the fast tempo of the advance, American logistics proved able to support the offensive. The use of Fedayeen irregulars, some of whom fought vigorously, did, however, lead to somewhat naive American complaints about such Iraqi tactics as disguise and fake surrender.

Much of the Republican Guard ran away in the face of American firepower. Units that redeployed or stood and fought were pulverised, with particular effort being devoted to destroying Iraqi artillery and armour. This effort represented the tactical and operational value of American air power. These tactical attacks accomplished more than the 'Shock and Awe' assault on Baghdad from the night of 19 March at the outset of the struggle, although the latter's impact on Iraqi command and control was significant. Moreover, had it occurred, the killing or wounding of Saddam Hussein in an air strike would have reflected the strategic value of air power in disrupting opposing leadership. Air power also brought a valuable dominance of reconnaissance. Thus, Coalition units were informed of the location of opposing Iraqi units, while it was difficult for the Iraqis to find targets, most obviously for their artillery, until they were engaged by them.

In their campaign, the Americans made particular use of JDAMS (Joint Direct Attack Munitions) which employed GPS to make conventional bombs act as satellite-guided weapons. This capability was an important addition to the improvement in American air-power capability that characterised post-Vietnam developments. Although there were differences of opinion between Britain and the USA over targeting, the air assault did not face the constraints that had affected the attack on the Serbs in Operation Allied Force in 1999. Instead, with a clear target, it was possible to use air power effectively and, in turn, to contribute to its reputation for effectiveness. About 70 per cent of the aerial munitions used were 'smart' or guided, rather than 'dumb' or unguided, in contrast to 10 per cent against Iraq in 1991.

The Americans also benefited from the use of helicopter gunships, especially the impressive AH-60 Apache, from Predator and Global Hawk unmanned aerial vehicles and from improvements in the accuracy of artillery fire. The Iraqi Russian-built T-55s, T-62s and, even, T-72s which were not destroyed by air attack, as many were, could not prevail against the American Abrams and the British Challenger II tanks (which were also able to resist rocket-propelled grenades), while the Americans' use of night-vision goggles enabled them to maintain the pace of the assault and, thus, to prevent the Iraqis from resupplying and regrouping. The Coalition armoured personnel carriers were also better than the Iraqi counterparts. More generally, the Americans benefited from intensive realistic training from the 1980s, while the British forces also proved well trained.

In turn, the Iraqis had good artillery and made effective use of rocket-propelled grenades, a dangerous enhancement to infantry firepower; but, although there had been improvements in Iraqi quality, as a honed-down force was sought, their military was far weaker than in 1991, in large part because the impact of international sanctions since then had limited the build-up of modern weaponry. Much of the weaponry was obsolete but more significant was a lack of morale and cohesion on the part of much of the regular army. Conscripted through intimidation, many in this army were disaffected Shias who were ready to desert. The destruction of the regime's grip proved a key element in encouraging mass desertion, with the troops melting into the population, a process aided by the degree to which much of the conflict occurred in the south, where the Shias were in a majority. In addition, the officer corps was demoralised. Some had plotted against the regime, which distrusted the army; relatively few had much time for it; and the collapse of the regime's grip increased the tendency towards disintegration.

The morale of the regulars had been lessened by the favour shown to the rival Republican Guard, a force of 50,000–60,000 troops who received better pay, food and equipment, but the Republican Guard also had varied loyalty and limited training, while its equipment had deteriorated in the 1990s, due to a lack of upgrading and adequate maintenance. The lack of training proved particularly serious and helped ensure that troops who were willing to die caused relatively few casualties among the Coalition forces. This situation was also true of the irregulars who had been built up into a force by Saddam's eldest son, Uday.

Once they had closed on Baghdad, the Americans launched, from 5 April, 'thunder runs', armoured thrusts into the city demonstrating that their opponents could not prevent these advances, and therefore undermining their position. In at least this case, manoeuvre warfare was thus shown to work in an urban context, and tanks proved able to destroy those who fought back. The lack of any real Iraqi attempt to use the very extensive urban cover offered by Baghdad helped the Americans. Having captured Baghdad, where organised resistance collapsed on 9 April, the Americans pressed on to overrun the rest of Iraq without encouraging the large-scale opposition that was feared, especially in Saddam Hussein's hometown of Tikrit, which fell on 14 April.

The British meanwhile had taken Basra, Iraq's second most populous city, which finally fell on 6–7 April, but were too heavily committed thereabouts to offer effective assistance further north. This success proved a striking contrast with the failures of repeated Iranian attacks on Basra, their key goal, during the war of 1980–8.

A prime element of debate before the campaign, which was revived during it when American supply lines came under serious attack, had related to the number of troops required for a successful invasion. The Secretary of Defense, Donald Rumsfeld, and other non-military commentators, had been encouraged by the rapid overthrow of the Taliban regime in Afghanistan in 2001 to argue that air power and special forces were the prime requirements for successful operations and that the large number of troops pressed for by the army leadership, for both the Iraq invasion and for subsequent occupation, was excessive. In the event, military pressure led to the allocation of sizeable numbers for the invasion of Iraq, but these were less numerous than those deployed in 1991.

Moreover, the 2003 campaign did not see the full committal of forces originally envisaged because the Turkish refusal to allow an invasion across its frontier with Iraq ensured that troops from the American 4th Infantry Division prepared for that invasion could not be used at the outset of the war. However, American Special Forces, landed by air from the night of 22–3 March, helped direct Kurdish pressure (and American bombing) on government forces in northern Iraq. Kurdish and American forces captured Kirkuk on 10 April, and, next day, Mosul surrendered. Concern that Turkey would complicate the situation by invading northern Iraq and clashing with the Kurds proved unfounded, while Iran also did not intervene. The failure of Iraq to fire its Saud missiles against Israel also ensured that the internationalisation of the conflict was limited.[9]

The consequences of the rapid fall of Iraq did, however, expose one of the problems with having insufficient troops in that it proved difficult to restore order and the workings of government. Too few troops had been dispatched, in part because of a conviction that American capability was such that only three divisions would be required and, in part, due to an underrating of the difficulty of securing internal support. The mass welcome in Iraq that had been anticipated, in large part as a result of a willingness to accept the promises of exiles, did not materialise. Rumsfeld indeed planned to redeploy much of the invasion force out of Iraq as soon as the invasion was over. There was also inadequate preparation for post-war disorder and division, not least widespread looting, a failure that was largely due to Rumsfeld and to misplaced confidence by him and his advisers.

These deficiencies were apparent prior to the invasion, not only to British planners but also in the USA. On 22 February 2003, the American National Defense University in the USA hosted an interagency planning conference, drawing on military planners and other specialists. They concluded that there were insufficient troops to stabilise Iraq after a successful invasion.[10] Three days later, General Eric Shinseki told a senate hearing that such stabilisation would require 'several hundred thousand troops', a figure that accorded with what General Tommy Franks had requested. Such views clashed with Rumsfeld's demand for a smaller military focused on war-winning, and not nation-building, and his confidence that the Pentagon need not plan for the latter as far as Iraq was concerned. Rumsfeld worked hard to keep the number of troops down, both before and after the war.

The collapse of the Iraqi regime led to American talk of pressing on to attack other states that harboured terrorism and were developing weapons of mass destruction, particularly Iran and Syria. Yet, the failure to restore order in Iraq and the costs of that commitment, in turn, swiftly fostered caution and led to a reaction against interventionism in this form. The situation in Iraq proved intractable, with American forces unable to fill the security vacuum left by the rapid and total collapse of the Baathist regime. Nor were they able to enforce a monopoly of force in a situation in which Iraqis competed for control of the new order. The

American decision to disband the Iraqi army and to push through a policy of de-Baathification helped rally support for Sunni insurrection. The capture of Saddam Hussein on 13 December 2003 made no difference. Part of the violence was directed against American forces, in what can be termed an insurgency, although it was in practice less coherent and more disorganised than such a term might suggest.

The insurgency developed just after the overthrow of the Saddam regime. It was related to greatly increased sectarian violence, verging at times on civil war, with Sunni–Shia differences intertwined with disputes over autonomy and oil revenues. In particular, many of the Sunnis were at best ambivalent about a democratic Iraq governing the entire country, which they saw in terms of rule by the majority Shia, whose backlash they feared. There was also a pronounced overlap between Sunni insurgent activity and straightforward criminality, not least in the propensity to resort to kidnapping. This overlap also made suppression of the insurgency particularly difficult.

In turn, the numerous Shia militias provided the Shia population with a degree of protection against the suicide bombings of Sunni extremists. There were also major differences within the Shia and Sunni communities. In part, these rivalries could be subsumed into wider themes by presenting them in terms of a clash between fundamentalism and moderation, but the situation was more complex. Clan, factional and personal ambitions all played a role, not least with the struggles between Shia militias to control branches of the state.

In response to attacks on some units, the American military, encouraged by Rumsfeld to anticipate a speedy departure, adopted a big-unit approach, with an emphasis on conventional tactics rather than on those appropriate for COIN. The stress on armour and air support provided firepower, and it proved possible to detain thousands of Iraqis in cordon-and-search operations, but this exacerbated resentment without winning support, and the prisoners anyway had to be released. British military observers felt American policy an inappropriate response, unlikely to win 'hearts and minds' as also, with time, did a growing number of American commentators.[11] In terms of a response reliant on force, there were insufficient troops as well as inappropriate tactics.

Problems were also created by shifts in American policy. The priorities rapidly moved from that of removing Saddam Hussein to establishing a liberal democracy that would bring stability and create a model for the Muslim world, indeed for a transformation of values and practices that would help anchor the international order. This highly ambitious plan was not only seriously unrealistic but also required a degree of peacefulness that made disorder a particular challenge and threat. In time, the Americans moved from this goal to that of extrication, but political exigencies within the USA were a powerful constraint, not least George W. Bush's determination to win re-election in November 2004 and subsequently his concern with 'legacy' issues.

Post-war disorder did not cease when the Americans handed over power to an Iraqi government in June 2004. Insurgents took over control of towns and were able to resist American and Iraqi attempts to drive them out. The insurgency drew not only on foreign volunteers but also on members of Saddam Hussein's forces who regrouped during the American occupation. The main challenge came from Shia activists, especially the large 'Mahdi Army' militia of the firebrand cleric Muqtada al-Sadr. This militia rebelled in April 2004 and took over the town of Najaf and held it against attack in August 2004.[12] Most resistance was faction-based. Looking to Iran for support, Shia militias were able to resist the new Iraqi army, so that the al-Maliki government, which took office in May 2006, was readier to accommodate itself to power within the Shia community than to confront it. The extent to which the Iraqi police was riddled with factions was also a major problem.

The situation on the ground was far from constant, and a 'surge' in American numbers in 2007, with the addition of 30,000 more combat troops, considerably eased the security situation, while also responding to the debate within the USA over policy. This 'surge' was designed to provide the opportunity to create an effective relationship between the Iraqi public and government, bypassing, in the process, both insurgents and independent militia. Yet, serious problems faced the attempt to create both security and a stable, pro-Western government, the two, of course, being closely intertwined in American aspirations. In August 2007, the Mahdi army withdrew from the streets, but it remained a powerful force in being and was able to resist to a considerable extent the efforts of the al-Maliki government to control its role. Looked at differently, rather than putting the emphasis on hostility, there is, in practice, considerable Iranian influence both in the ministries of the government and amongst the militia. Thus, in March 2008, Iran brokered a ceasefire in Basra, ending a government attempt to reduce militia influence in the city. In June 2008, however, an American–Iraqi move to take over the city of Amarah succeeded. The city had been handed over by the British to the Iraqi army in 2006, but the latter had then been unable to prevent occupation by the Mahdi army.

More generally, the US forces appeared to be successful in sponsoring the formation of 'concerned local citizen', later called 'Sons of Iraq', groups – neighbourhood militias that would contribute to stability. Whereas, earlier, Iraqi support for the US-backed government had been from some sections of the Shia community, many of these groups were Sunnis, and their action represented a choice against the chaos and brutality of al-Qaeda-linked terrorists. The USA also negotiated with former insurgent groups such as the 1920 Revolution Brigades. Al-Qaeda brutality, for example the killing of tribal leaders and the forcible recruitment of suicide bombers, had alienated much Sunni support for al-Qaeda, and this had strategic consequences.

This brutality received far less attention in the West than occasional and unauthorised brutalities by Coalition forces, as in the Abu-Ghraib prison. The respective degree of attention devoted to the two types of brutality is highly instructive, for Western self-criticism, while praiseworthy, also leads to a marked failure to appreciate typicality and proportionality. At the same time, an understanding of failures on the part of Coalition forces, however atypical these failures may be, is important when considering popular attitudes.

The sponsoring of allied forces by the USA was an aspect of 'the surge' which was successful, as was the negative goal of thwarting civil war. The USA understood that it had to operate in response to Iraq's sectarian divides. By creating a shared constituency with the Sunnis, the Americans reduced their own dependence on the Shia and gave the latter more reason to compromise and, thus, to accommodate Sunni interests. In turn, the Sunnis were provided with a way to abandon the insurgency. There were parallels here with British policy in Northern Ireland in the 1990s. The key goal was to try to differentiate among opponents and to create the basis for compromise with some of them.

As a military correlate, there was an emphasis on information-driven operations, especially raids, rather than on the larger-scale application of force. In particular, there was an attempt to regain the initiative from the insurgents, especially by killing their leaders and attacking their safe havens and logistical bases. In place of raid and return, the emphasis for the Coalition forces was on moving troops among the people, to heighten confidence and a sense of security. This emphasis reflected a more appropriate doctrine, as well as improved training and tactics. Thus, a more pragmatic politics was accompanied by more pertinent tactics. Four years too late of course, but better than nothing and also showing the capacity of the military to change and develop, a capacity that places a question mark against the commonplace comments about inherent national cultural military styles.

More specifically, the challenge of operations in Iraq affected the balance between and within American arms. There was a stronger emphasis, as a result of these operations, on current and likely future roles for infantry and special forces and a decline in the role allocated for armour and artillery. Instead, armour and artillery units were sent to Iraq without their equipment and were expected to act as infantry there: the case for three-quarters of the American armoured units sent. This practice hit training and familiarisation with weaponry and aroused concern among commanders. Ironically, the increased use by insurgents of improvised roadside bombs and the serious damage they inflicted on infantry ensured that it became necessary to increase the armoured protection of ordinary troop transports and armoured personnel carriers. While not tanks, the results were a reminder of the need to combine protection with mobility.

Aside from problems in Iraq, the wider political and geopolitical equations moved against the USA as it found itself entangled in a crisis that lessened its options elsewhere. The issue was played out in American politics, with the Bush administration emphasising the need to stay the course, but this was as part of an increasingly pessimistic prospectus in which the stress was on extrication and on leaving Iraq to the Iraqis. Compared with hopes in 2003, this stress represented a more limited definition of success which, indeed, may be an aspect of modern warfare. In addition, the American ability to act elsewhere had been lessened, politically, financially and in terms of the armed force available. Thus, there was no military intervention to stop genocide in the Darfur region of Sudan (see pp. 90–1).

The Iraq war led the Americans to devote renewed effort to their already vigorous debate about force structure and tasking. At the risk of considerable simplification, this located discussion about weaponry within consideration of the continued validity of a military centred on separate services. Rumsfeld was particularly keen on breaking with what he perceived as a conservative inheritance advocated strongly by the army out of line with what he saw as the need for rapidly delivered force. Interest in new weaponry focused on AirLand combinations but included research into space weapons systems as well as on low-yield nuclear weaponry which was seen as an important way to upgrade America's nuclear capability.

Meanwhile, due in part to the Iraq commitment, defence expenditure rose – from 276 billion dollars in 1998 to 310 billion dollars in 2001. Moreover, America's share of world military expenditure was very high. In 2000, the USA spent 295 billion dollars compared to a figure for Russia and China combined of 100 billion dollars. The 2001 figure was more than the next nine largest national military budgets combined, while, for 2002, the sum was about 40 per cent of the world's total military spending, although expectations of, and costs for, items such as pay, food and social benefits varied greatly across the world. This expenditure, however, does not necessarily translate into lower effectiveness for the high spenders, as attractive conditions and high morale help with recruitment and the crucial issue of retention. By 2007, the USA was spending 450 billion dollars a year, including 275 million dollars daily on Iraq. As an instance of the less threatening atmosphere prior to the War on Terror, William Cohen, the Secretary of Defense, had called in February 1999 for spending to reach 318.9 billion dollars by 2005. The total cost of the Iraq war and subsequent occupation is a matter of controversy, and much of it does not appear on the military budget, not least as a result of the outsourcing represented by the large-scale use of contractors. By 2007, there were about 100,000 contractors in Iraq, including 35,000 with explicit private-security commitments. Contractors have suffered the second-largest number of Coalition casualties in Iraq – after the American military, but more than its British counterpart. A recent study suggested that the costs, for the USA, of the Iraq and Afghanistan conflicts ranged between 2.2 trillion dollars and 5 trillion dollars.[13]

Manpower strains were also a serious issue. Possibly the attacks in 2001 represented an opportunity for a mobilisation of opinion within the USA behind a new commitment to public service, notably in the National Guard, and even a degree of conscription, or the far easier alternative of the expansion of army strength through improved pay. That, however, was not the route taken by the Bush government, not least due to its commitment to Transformation, and normal political services and procurement policies rapidly resumed. This situation helped ensure that the manpower available was put under enormous pressure by the addition of the long-term commitments in Afghanistan and Iraq to existing obligations. For example, in March 2006 there were 138,000 American troops in Iraq.

Lengthened tours of service affected morale and thus retention in both the army and the National Guard and, breaching Pentagon guidelines, reduced the time available for training. Nevertheless, the determination of the military remained apparent. Polls indicated declining support for the war among the army, but, while this influenced retention, it was not pushed towards public disaffection. For example, in 2006, Lieutenant Ehren Watada refused to serve in Iraq on the grounds that the war was 'not only morally wrong but a horrible breach of American law'; but this was very much an isolated stance. Similar manpower issues affected Britain and Canada.

Repeated tours increased experience of COIN warfare. For example, American troops gained experience in how to counter IEDs (improvised explosive devices). They developed relevant technology, such as jammers designed to thwart remote triggers for IEDs, as well as relevant tactics. These tactics were not only defensive but also offensive, for example the deployment of snipers near likely spots. In turn, the insurgents used larger bombs as well as their own snipers, creating a new front line. IEDs became a major problem not only in Iraq but also in Afghanistan. Suicide car bombs were also employed in both against Western forces and their local allies.

In Iraq, the Americans were able, not least thanks to their 'surge' in troops numbers in 2007 (by which time they were spending 54 billion dollars annually to support their military operations in Iraq), as well as their building up of a new Iraqi army and police, to improve the security situation considerably, but this situation was scarcely stable. Nor was there the hoped-for political and economic progress. Moreover, much depended on the willingness of hostile Iranian-linked Shia militias to draw back from confronting the Americans. Instead, in pursuit of power, they focused on conflict with each other, while the American-backed government enjoyed only limited power.

As with Afghanistan, what, from the Western perspective, can be viewed as an inability to create effective peace-making that contrasted with the initial military victory can also be seen in terms of a more continual process of conflict. In this process, peacekeeping, instead, has to be understood as an attempt to contain counter-attacks. This situation thus brings together two very different military narratives, with the equations of Western power, such as kill ratios or troop density, only being of limited value.

Although no other power could match American expenditure, the impact of American weaponry in Iraq in 2003, and the claims that it ushered in a new age of warfare, encouraged interest elsewhere in procuring similar weapons. This situation was true, for example, of Britain and Israel, in each of which the development of drones was stepped up, and also of Japan, which felt increasingly threatened by North Korean rocketry. This fear led to Japanese interest in anti-missile defences and in satellite surveillance.

Japan launched its own spy satellites in 2003. Article 9 of the Japanese Constitution states that 'land, sea, and air forces, as well as other war potential, will never be maintained.' As a result, Japan has 'Self-Defence Forces' (SDF), which were 258,000 strong in 2003, making it one of the most powerful militaries in the world. Nevertheless, the 1992 law authorising the SDF to deploy abroad included strict restrictions on what it could do: it could only be sent to areas where a ceasefire was in place. SDF troops were sent to help UN peacekeepers in Cambodia (1992), Mozambique (1993) and East Timor (1999 and 2002), to help Rwandan refugees (1994) and to assist in peacekeeping in Iraq after the Second Gulf War.

Cruise missiles attracted greater international interest after their large-scale use in Iraq in 2003. The following year, there was speculation that a Chinese invasion of Taiwan would be countered by a Taiwanese Cruise-missile attack on the Three Gorges Dam in the Yangzi Valley, exploiting a key point of economic and environmental vulnerability. The same year, Australia agreed to spend up to 450 million dollars on buying air-launched Cruise missiles with a range of at least 250 kilometres (150 miles). The Chinese *Shang*-class nuclear attack submarines which are currently entering service will be able to deploy land-attack Cruise missiles as well as anti-ship Cruise missiles.

A continual process of innovation was an aspect of the procurement process, and the Cruise missile was far from alone in this. In 2006, for example, the American air force conducted tests in which aircraft used synthetic fuel as part of their jet fuel. Moreover, stealth technology was increasingly applied to aircraft, for example to the Joint Strike Fighter developed by the USA and other partners including Australia.

The development of satellite capability by Japan was one response by a power employing advanced military systems, while India used the threat of terrorism to justify the Prevention of Terrorism Ordinance promulgated in October 2001.[14] Israel faced more immediate problems. Indeed, albeit in very different contexts, developments in Afghanistan (see pp. 86–9), Iraq and Israel in the mid-2000s indicated the problems facing advanced militaries using the latest technology when confronted by insurrectionary movements employing guerrilla tactics and terrorist methods.

Negotiations between Israel and the Palestinians at Camp David had broken down in 2000 over the issues of Israeli settlements on the West Bank of the Jordan, Arab demands that refugees, many from 1948, be allowed to return to Israel – the so-called 'right of return' – and the status of Jerusalem. On 27 September 2000, the visit of Ariel Sharon, then leader of the opposition Likud Party, to the Haram al-Sharif, the holiest Muslim shrine in Jerusalem, in the al-Aqsa compound on the Temple Mount, led to Palestinian demonstrations and a forcible Israeli response in which Palestinians were killed. Violence fed more violence on both sides, with Arab attacks on Israeli civilians leading to what rapidly became a more violent rising than the first intifada. The combination of Arab rejectionism at Camp David and the violence of the new intifida encouraged Israeli public opinion to regard peace talks as a failed option.

Winning power in February 2001, in part by rejecting the idea of land cessions without peace talks, Sharon promised to increase the number of settlements in the occupied territories, and, the following month, suicide bombers were used by Hamas (Harakat al-Muqawama al-Islamiyya; Islamic Resistance Movement). Israeli operations in the West Bank and Gaza indicated the limitations of Israeli military and political options: the killing of militant leaders did not stop attacks, while Israel found it difficult to foster the creation of a Palestinian constituency for effective negotiations. Equally, the attitudes and policies of the Palestinian government of Yasser Arafat made negotiations difficult. In response to continued attacks by suicide bombers, the Israelis began construction of a security wall designed to seal off the West Bank except through checkpoints and thus to block such suicide attacks. Sharon also switched to the very policy he had rejected, unilateral withdrawal, the policy followed by the Labour government under Ehud Barak, a former general, when Israel evacuated its 'security zone' in southern Lebanon in 2000. In 2005, the Israelis evacuated the Gaza Strip, and the army was used to force obdurate Jewish settlers to leave their settlements.

The use of rockets, however, ensured that Israel's hopes of clear borders and of employing fixed defences, such as walls, to provide protection appeared otiose; although, more positively, they were largely designed to provide checkpoints that would limit vulnerability to suicide bombers. In 2004, the wall between Israel and the occupied territories appeared to reduce the rate of suicide attacks; but, nevertheless, they continued, as did Israeli reprisals. Thus, in September 2004, Israel launched a missile strike that killed fourteen Hamas activists in Gaza in response to a double suicide bombing in Beersheba that had killed sixteen Israelis. A ceasefire was agreed in February 2005.

The Israeli failure to win much Arab backing, a failure underlined by Hamas's success in the Palestinian Council elections of 2006, was a more serious challenge, but one that exposed the absence, in the case of Israel, of the necessary political dimension for any COIN campaign. Neither Israel, nor the Palestinians, nor outside powers, notably the Quartet that sought a negotiated settlement, were able to secure politically the goal of a viable Palestinian state alongside a secure Israel. This failure provided the background to acts of violence on both sides that served little point other than underlining the absence of stability and the reliance on a politics of reprisal.

Israel suffered from its inability to determine developments among other players, especially the ability of Hamas to take over control of the Gaza Strip. Israel was not able to prevent this and thus became far more vulnerable to short-range rocket attacks mounted by Islamic Jihad, a group Hamas did not hinder. The Israeli use of tank incursions in response proved of limited value.

A parallel case operated on Israel's northern border where Hizbullah consolidated its power in southern Lebanon and mounted attacks from there on Israel. In response, and more particularly to a Hizbullah ambush on 12 July 2006 of an Israeli unit patrolling the frontier, Israel decided to destroy Hizbullah's military power and capacity, especially its leadership and its large and dangerous rocket arsenal. To that end, Israel blockaded Lebanon and launched a large-scale limited invasion that month, combined with extensive aerial attack, focused in particular on rocket sites. This offensive, however, proved misconceived and poorly executed. Several of the Israeli Merkava tanks fell victim to Hizbullah use of large roadside explosive devices, and this tactical problem was an aspect of the degree to which the Israeli desire for movement and speed had to confront the exigencies of position warfare. Moreover, the Israeli air assault failed to crush resistance and, instead, wreaked a degree of devastation on Lebanon's civilian population that challenged Israel's international reputation and helped ensure that Israel lost the information war.

Hizbullah, in turn, fired about 5,000 rockets, dramatically confounding Israel's capacity for deterrence. Close to one million Israelis moved south away from exposed frontier areas or took shelter in air-raid shelters. Haifa, the key city in the north, was particularly exposed. Public criticism rose, but, on the other hand, civilian resolve was not crushed. Both sides used drones, with the Israelis making particularly marked use of them as an instance of their aerial dominance and attack capacity. Hizbullah's drones had been provided by Iran, which uses its oil wealth to fund the movement, supplying it via Syria and thus benefiting from Syria's position in Lebanon. Israeli air power proved unable to end rocket attacks from Lebanon, although a large percentage of the long-range Hizbullah rocket systems were destroyed.

The difficulties encountered by Israel, however, indicated the contrast between force projection and military output (which missiles have greatly enhanced) and, on the other hand, being able to predict and force a successful resolution of the crisis. During the crisis, Israel had about 150 fatalities (120 soldiers, thirty civilians), and Hizbullah had 500–700 dead. There was no sense of achievement in Israel, which Sharon had earlier declared a regional superpower, and the Defence Minister during the war, Amir Peretz, was defeated when he stood for leader of the Labour Party in 2007. A sense of anger in Israel was seen in media criticism during the war and in the establishment by the government of the Winograd Commission to investigate the conduct of the conflict.

Reporting in early 2008, the Commission found poor preparation and inappropriate strategy. In part, this strategy had rested on a failure to understand the extent to which Hizbullah had become more effective, making expectations about Israeli success unrealistic. Leaving aside the misguided nature of the assumption that problems could be overcome simply by the use of force, there was a failure to understand the relative military balance at the tactical, operational and strategic levels.

The major role of the international context was abundantly demonstrated by the Lebanon crisis of 2006, as the USA provided Israel with support in the face of considerable international criticism, while Syria and Iran were willing to rearm Hizbullah after the conflict, breaching the arms embargo ordered by the UN under Resolution 1701. Hizbullah boasted that its entire military system was rapidly re-established. In addition, Hizbullah built up an even stronger rocket capacity, ensuring a potent offensive threat to Israel, and one that could be mounted from behind strengthened anti-tank and anti-aircraft defence systems. This rocket capacity may well lead to a resumption of Israeli attack.[15] Iran, which finances Hizbullah, appears to see Hizbullah's strength as a deterrent to Israeli action against Iran's nuclear programme. In the meanwhile, although Israel did not regard itself as defeated, Hizbullah's proclaimed ability to resist Israel markedly increased its symbolic capital and its prestige within the radical world, ensuring more support from rejectionist powers and groups.[16] This support was an aspect of Hizbullah's ability to shape the information domain, an ability also directed against Israeli public confidence, with television footage being broadcast of Israeli casualties.[17] More generally, the continued strength of Hizbullah and its role as a force for regional instability was displayed in 2008 in its successful confrontation with the Lebanese government.

At the same time, the complexity of international alignments was indicated by Iran's pleasure in Hamas's ability to seize the Gaza Strip from the Fatah-dominated Palestinian government in June 2007, and yet also its role in supporting the Shia-dominated Iraqi government, which was also America's basis for stability in the country. Moreover, in 2008, in the aftermath of Israel's September 2007 attack on Syrian nuclear facilities, Syria and Israel sought to develop a modus vivendi. Israel's air exercises in June 2008 seem to have been intended as a practice for an attack on Iran's considerably more extensive nuclear facilities.

As a reminder of the range of circumstances in which Western powers could experience difficulties, France, from 2002, found that its commitment in its former colony of Ivory Coast, an important economic power which had hitherto been stable, encountered serious problems due to the interaction of ethnic with religious tensions that led to a bitter civil war in 2002–4. These problems were a marked qualification of the habitual French ability to direct the affairs of most of its former colonies, an ability supported by bases in the Central African Republic, Chad, Djibouti, Gabon, Ivory Coast and Senegal.

The capability of advanced military powers seemed more brittle by 2008 than had been the case six years earlier. This shift was important not only to military history but also to the politics of the modern world and the future of war. There is also a challenge for analysts. It is easy to see a contrast between what is presented as an apogee of a Western model of war-making and opposition by the representatives of non-Western systems; but there is a need to be wary of presenting in cultural and geographical terms what is in part a more widespread military practice, within as well as between systems, namely the response of the weaker power in an asymmetric relationship.[18] This response classically focuses on developing an anti-strategy, anti-operational method, anti-tactics and anti-weaponry, designed to counter and lessen, if not nullify, the advantages of the stronger.

Yet, to focus on fighting may be to ignore the degree to which, and for both sides, the fighting was only part of the equation of conflict. Instead, the emphasis was on affecting the will of the other side, of exploiting its vulnerabilities and of lessening its willingness to fight. Sometimes referred to as 'hearts and minds', this was a strategy pursued by both Western and non-Western combatants, although the emphasis varied greatly. Western powers and their allies sought to win support or, at least, acquiescence in Afghanistan, Iraq, Lebanon and Palestine, while their opponents both resisted this process at the local level and tried to undermine domestic resolve in the Western home populations. This process entailed two very different issues. On the one hand, there was the struggle with Muslim extremism, both in the Muslim world in South Asia and among Muslim communities in the West, and, on the other, the battle for opinion within Western majority communities. Fighting on the ground was mediated through these different perspectives, but, in turn, the latter were as much, if not more, affected by other aspects of the politics of the conflict. Real or alleged violations of the rights of terrorist suspects, for example, played a role, as, more generally, did the politics of incarceration.

For Western powers, the battle of opinion in part involves resisting subversion. Indeed, the latter can be seen as the most effective form of insurrection. Thus, the war on terror centrally involves opposition to attitudes that countenance radical Islam, and this entails soft power more than the military capability that has also to be available. Such points were not at the forefront of military commentary in the 1990s but have become far more prominent.

Doctrine has been affected, with much attention to COIN doctrines, as with the American army and the Marine Corps' Field Manual 3–24, *Counter Insurgency,* published in December 2006. Secondary literature has also plundered supposedly relevant historical episodes,[19] although the extent to which comparisons can be drawn is unclear. In particular, it is necessary to understand the extent to which insurgencies (like irregular warfare) vary and have the capacity to develop. This emphasis on variety and development is also relevant to the nature of COIN warfare, which has itself to respond dynamically to changing circumstances; as indeed the Americans have done in Iraq, in both situational awareness and response.[20]

This situation poses particular problems for force structure, doctrine and training, as these needs are considerable in COIN warfare. John McGarth's historically grounded study of troop density suggests a need for 'about 13.26 troops per 1000 inhabitants', the 13.26 including indigenous police and military, as well as contractors, and he argues that indigenous units and contractor forces were among the key factors in troop density in Iraq.[21] As a result, the insurgents, finding American targets very difficult, devoted much effort to assaults on the police (as in Mosul in November 2004), which, in turn, encouraged the formation of police commando units, which played key roles in both combat and control. This analysis therefore directs attention to the political factors that affected the viability of relying on indigenous units, as well as the extent to which it was necessary (as well as desirable) for the world's strongest military in its prime field of commitment to rely on such units as well as on contractors.

The post-2003 situation in Iraq underlines broader questions about the reliance on COIN, for, aside from the practicality of COIN operations in particular contexts, it might well be unusual in the future to be able to achieve such a focus in commitments. More generally, military and political practicality and viability are issues whether or not the intention is in part to rely on allies. The costs to the USA, financial and political, of the Iraq commitment after 2003 also raise the question of whether a long-term 'militarisation' of a political situation is desirable even if victory, however defined, can be won. In short, does recent discussion of the best doctrine for COIN miss the point as the cost is too high, or is this only the case in terms of the particular circumstances and specifications of the Iraq crisis? Taking the example of that crisis, how many Operation al-Fajrs (Operation New Dawns), the hard-fought cleaning of the insurgent stronghold of Fallujah in late 2004, could be afforded by the USA or other powers? Turned round, however, despite their rhetoric, insurgent numbers were, and are, not unlimited, and focusing conflict on particular clashes could weaken them greatly and break the impression of insurgent success. Moreover, 'if the enemy center of gravity was their leadership', then that could be disrupted or destroyed.[22] Thus, military action could prove a direct part of the political solution.

Furthermore, there is the more general point, that lack of success is not, as it may seem, the definition of failure, as that may set too high a benchmark for justifying action. Indeed, the very commitment of troops may prevent a more serious situation, as with British army operations in Northern Ireland or, very differently, the dispatch of American National Guard troops to the Mexican border in 2006 to help the Border Patrol limit illegal immigration.[23] Possibly this is the most important conclusion. The use of force may produce a situation that is analogous to that of the police – limiting not ending crime – and may lead to a stasis that provides the context for eventual political discussion and negotiation.

CHAPTER 5

A MULTITUDE OF CONFLICTS

The problems of the Western militaries reflected the bringing together of the two narratives of warfare discussed in Chapters 2 and 3. In the 2000s, these narratives also continued to have a separate existence, and this chapter focuses on Third World conflict that did not so directly involve the major powers. At the same time, there was an important overlap.

This was abundantly demonstrated in the linked cases of Pakistan and Afghanistan after the fall of the Taliban in 2001. If there was not chaos in Afghanistan comparable to that in Liberia, this was only because the weakness of Hamid Karzai's central government was counterpointed by the strength of provincial governors, such as Abdul Rashid Dostum, Atta Mohammed, Gulbuddin Hekmatyar and Ismail Khan. These, however, were autonomous figures, whose tradition of independence was supported by their own armies which, like those of local militias, were powerful. For example, in 2004, the militia in the northern city of Kunduz had a considerable force of tanks. Rivalry between these warlords – over local dominance and revenue sources such as land and drug profits – was disruptive and led to conflict, for example between Abdul Rashid Dostum and Atta Mohammed near Mazar-e Sharif in late 2003 and in 2004.

Government in Afghanistan indeed involved a process of negotiation with these warlords, a process that accepted their regional power. Peace, in turn, depended on their restraint, but it was threatened by challenges to the regional position of warlords, as well as to that of the central government. A Taliban resurgence led, however, to the collapse of the government position in much of the south and east of the country, with the President, who had not been able to consolidate the new order, wielding scant authority outside the capital.

This resurgence, which gathered pace in 2005, was the cause of renewed Western intervention in the shape of NATO forces from 2006. The resurgence, however, gravely challenged not only the ineffective and in part corrupt Karzai government but also the NATO forces deployed to support it. This was particularly the case for the British forces in Helmand Province, but also in Kandahar where the Canadians suffered badly from a resistance that was stronger than anticipated, with the Taliban benefiting greatly from assistance from across the Pakistani frontier. More generally, Taliban forces were more numerous and better led, trained and organised than they had been in 2002.

More specific problems for the British in Helmand included the terrain: far from being desert, in which the British could employ their superior firepower, their units found themselves deployed in small settlements where walls and orchards provided cover for Taliban assailants. The British were also greatly handicapped by a shortage of helicopters. This shortage lessened their firepower and hit both mobility and logistics. Frequently pushed onto the defensive as a result, the British were therefore exposed to Taliban attacks, while the shortage of air mobility led to a use of road links that led to casualties from roadside bombs.

Moreover, the supporting Pakistani military deployment, first in 2001, and then from 2003 in Waziristan in the Federally Administered Tribal Areas (FATA) did not succeed in destroying the Taliban bases in the region, despite American air and financial support, as well as training. Instead, the Pakistani military, despite deploying 80,000 troops, encountered fierce resistance, both from the Taliban and from much of the local population and proved unable to hold the initiative or dominate the situation. After what was seen as unacceptable casualties, and was certainly failure, the Pakistani military withdrew in 2006, and the Taliban were left able to enjoy the shelter of the region. Furthermore, in October 2006, the army agreed a peace with the tribal leaders that accepted this status quo, although the tribes promised to evict foreigners from their areas. Support for the Taliban from within Pakistan, not least from elements of the Frontier Force, remains important. There were NATO complaints, especially from the Americans, about the Pakistani government, and its complicity with the Taliban, and these appear to have been justified, at least in so far as the ISI was concerned. Conversely, a standard Pakistani view was that Karzai lacked legitimacy, not least because he was seen as an American puppet.

At a very different scale to the problems posed by Pakistan, many of the NATO forces operating in Afghanistan themselves insisted on 'national caveats' restricting what their forces could do. The resulting rules of engagement proved very varied, which hit at the idea of interoperability. The Germans proved particularly reluctant to make an active contribution in conflict scenarios.

As elsewhere, the 'international' dimension has to be supplemented by a domestic one. Thus, in the FATA, the socio-political structure was also at stake. The Taliban supporters were largely outside the mainstream of traditional tribal structures. Instead, the supporters' leaders were not tribal elders. Moreover, clerics were prominent in the leadership of the Taliban supporters, a practice at variance with the traditional ethos in which mullahs were below such elders. Thus, the struggle by Taliban supporters was waged not only in Afghanistan, and in the North-West Frontier Province against Pakistani forces, but also against the traditional tribal leadership. The struggle in Pakistan was not restricted to the North-West Frontier Province but spread across Pakistan, with suicide bombers attacking the military from the spring of 2007.

The October 2006 'peace accord' in the FATA came to an end the following March in part because of the American rocket attack on a village seen as a militant hideout where the casualties included women and children. Within Afghanistan itself, the security situation markedly deteriorated from 2006, with Taliban operations becoming far more active and prominent.[1] This pressure tested somewhat complacent British assumptions that their military was more successful than the Americans at COIN operations.[2] Indeed, the British deployment in Helmand Province was characterised initially by foolish political grandstanding not only about the likely peaceful consequences but also about the military's ability to understand and control the situation. Tony Blair told British troops in 2006, 'here in this extraordinary desert is where the future of world security in the early twenty-first century is going to be played out.'

In practice, British forces were in part reduced to the militarised response, without any adequate political strategy, for which they habitually criticised the Americans. The Taliban proved able to put the British under considerable pressures, which, in turn, exposed problems with British weaponry and air–land coordination.[3] In both Britain and the USA, there was talk of the difficulty of fighting two wars at once (Iraq and Afghanistan). This argument was reasonable in terms of force numbers and deployments, but, irrespective of the Iraq commitment, there was a more fundamental problem in Afghanistan of being able both to win and to stabilise the victory, and each in adverse circumstances, not least with Pakistan a source of renewed opposition and Taliban resupply. The latter helped explain the military importance of the interdiction of crossing points, not least in the winter of 2007–8, but the political problem posed by Pakistan was not thereby addressed.

Angola, in contrast, was no longer at the forefront of international attention and confrontation. Nor was it a failed state. Yet, until the killing of the UNITA leader, Jonas Savimbi, in 2002, Angola faced a debilitating insurrectionary war that rested on ethnic tension, especially Ovimbundu support for UNITA, and was financed by exploitation of the country's diamond wealth. Diamonds were also important in financing conflict in West Africa, especially in Sierra Leone. In turn, the Angolan government benefited greatly from control of the country's oil.

Having rejected the results of the 1992 election, UNITA had resumed its conflict with the government, which was now weakened by the withdrawal of the Cuban and Soviet assistance that had greatly helped it in the civil war of the 1970s and 1980s. Defeated by the scale of the country, neither side was able to win. The operational effectiveness of the government's conventional forces declined in the wet season, which, in turn, favoured UNITA's guerrilla tactics. Each side mounted attacks on the supply systems of the other, which indeed were important to their effectiveness, but without lasting effect, other than to cause large numbers of civilian casualties and even larger numbers of refugees.

However, international pressure and a failure to win led Savimbi to negotiate anew in 1994, producing a de-facto partition of the country that lasted until 1997 when the government attacked UNITA. UNITA now suffered from both the loss of its supply route through Congo, where Mobutu had fallen, and from divisions, with Savimbi's leadership under challenge. In 1999, the government mounted intensive attacks, with Russian-made planes, on UNITA bases. It was claimed that they employed napalm and defoliants in addition to conventional explosives. Jamba, where Savimbi had established his capital in 1984, and which the government had failed to take in the 1980s, finally fell. UNITA forces were in a poor position by 2001, and the government used its oil wealth to enhance its military capability. The killing of Savimbi, on 22 February 2002, was rapidly followed, on 4 April, by the signature of a peace agreement.

A different type of attempted consolidation of central control over tribal groups and peripheral areas was seen in Sudan. Its government, which was made more intractable by the rise of militant Islam and by its links with Iran, confronted the long-standing issue of control over the south. The Comprehensive Peace Agreement, a peace deal with the Sudan People's Liberation Movement, taking them into government, and agreeing that in 2011 the south could decide on secession, was agreed in 2005, although tension continued. Rising oil revenues made this more pressing and became a cause of specific tension, with oil extraction in the south supported by Sudanese troops leading to considerable damage: vital cattle died from drinking contaminated water. In turn, there were attacks on the oil workers.

The government also faced a serious rebellion in the west. Dating to the 1970s, but breaking out with greater intensity in 2003, and mounted by the Sudan Liberation Army based in the Darfur region, this was directed against the oppression of non-Arabs by the government. In response, from 2004, the government used its regular forces, including aircraft and infantry moved in trucks, to support an Arab militia, the Janjaweed (many of whom rode on horses and camels), in order to slaughter the Fur, Masalit and, in particular, Zaghawa: native tribes in Darfur. Alongside large-scale slaughter, especially of men and boys, even very young boys, and the systematic rape and mutilation of women, natives were driven away, their cattle and therefore livelihood seized, the wells poisoned with corpses, and dams, pumps and buildings destroyed. The government was assisted by serious divisions among the opposition in Darfur, not least over negotiations and also over whether the goal was partition or a different Sudan. Militarily, the government benefited from its control over the central point of the capital, Khartoum, from the funds gained from resource exploitation, especially of oil, which enabled it to buy Chinese and Russian arms, and from its use of air power and artillery. The conflict in Sudan spilled over into Chad and the Central African Republic. Chad accused Sudan of backing rebels, and, in response, Chad forces crossed the border into Darfur in April 2007 and fought Sudanese troops.

Ethnic rivalry played a role in internal conflict in many other African states, although often without attracting much international attention, for example in northern Mali in 2004. More prominently, the Muslim north of Ivory Coast felt disenfranchised by the government elected in 2000 which was dominated by the Christian south. A rising in 2002 led to the seizure of the north by rebels and to serious fighting until 2004, followed by an agreement in 2007 that left Guillaume Soro, the leader of the rebel New Forces, as Prime Minister. In turn, there were divisions on the rebel side, including fighting in 2004. UN and French peacekeepers played a role in trying to contain the crisis.

As a stage between Afghanistan and Angola, Congo (formerly Zaire) became both a failed state and one in which regular forces from other African countries intervened in order to influence the direction of conflict there, to dominate neighbouring areas and to obtain control over raw materials (see pp. 50–1). Mobutu Sese Soko, the dictator since 1965, and a former general, fell in 1997 as a result of foreign invasion, while another invasion was launched in 1998 in an unsuccessful attempt to overthrow his replacement, Laurent Kabila. Uganda and Rwanda supported competing rebel factions, Rwanda in part in order to defeat the Hutu militias that staged the genocide of 1994 and that had taken refuge in Congo. In turn, Zimbabwe, Angola, Chad and Namibia backed Kabila, in part in response to the dynamics of their own internal security situations but also hoping to benefit from resources they could obtain. Angola wished to stop Congolese support for UNITA, which had been important under Mobutu. The outside powers armed their own Congolese allies, particularly, for Rwanda, the Rally for Congolese Democracy and the Union of Congolese Patriots. These overlapped with tribal militia groups, such as those of the Ugandan-backed Lendus, who competed with the Rwandan-allied Hemas in the north-eastern province of Ituri, a major centre of conflict.

Probably between 3.1 and 5.4 million people died in Congo between 1998 and 2003, most of disease and starvation, but many of them in ethnic conflict between tribal militias, as murderous attacks on villages proved a particularly common means of waging war. Far from being at the cutting edge of 'new-generation' warfare, this conflict saw much of the killing with machetes, and bows and arrows and shotguns were employed, alongside the frequent use of mortars and submachine guns. The conflict also led to cannibalism, as well as to the use of child warriors seen in West Africa, Uganda and Nepal, and by the Taliban in Afghanistan. Other aspects of African conflict which were distant from Western warfare included the use of traditional charms and spirit mediums.

Violence continued in Congo after the war officially ended in 2003 when the leading rebel groups joined a transitional government. Moreover, the violence continued to be brutal and symbolic. In the Katanga region in 2004, insurgents reputedly cut off the genitals of victims and drank their blood. Congo's first democratic election, in 2006, was seen as a possible harbinger of change, but the new government has found force a ready response to discontent, while there are also serious security problems with militias, especially in the provinces of North and South Kivu on the eastern border.

More generally, rivalries between states interacted with insurrections and other civil conflicts elsewhere. Thus, warfare between Eritrea and Ethiopia, which involved large-scale fighting of a conventional type, spilled over into internal conflicts in Somalia. In November 2006, the Prime Minister of Ethiopia called Islamists in Somalia a 'clear and present danger' to Ethiopia, a Christian state, claiming that they were being armed by Eritrea. In turn, the Somali Islamists, the Islamic Courts Union, met at Mogadishu and declared that they would defend Somalia against a 'reckless and war-thirsty' Ethiopia. Both Eritrea and Ethiopia sent troops into Somalia. Local struggles such as this one were interpreted by outside powers in terms of alleged wider alignments not only regional but also global, such as the struggle between the USA and Muslim fundamentalists. Thus, in Somalia in 2006, warlord resistance to the fundamentalist attempt to capture Mogadishu was covertly supported by the USA, although, in the event, the capital fell that June to the Islamic Courts Union and the forces of the latter pressed on to attack the Somali transitional government which had taken refuge in the town of Baidoa.

In turn, the American government encouraged the Ethiopian invasion that overthrew the Union and captured Mogadishu in the winter of 2006–7. For the USA, this was a welcome opportunity to benefit from regional animosities, and to leave the military work on the ground to local forces, although the Americans did provide some air support. Subsequently, opposition in Somalia to the Ethiopian-backed transitional government of Abdullahi Yusuf continued and became more clearly linked to fundamentalists, notably to the *Shabab* (young men) who sought to overthrow it. The *Shabab* were a continuation of the militias that had supported the Union. Al-Qaeda also played a role. At the same time, the opposition lacked the benefits enjoyed by the Taliban in Afghanistan, notably a largely safe haven in neighbouring Pakistan and the experience gained by several years of relatively constant conflict.

The problem of relating all conflicts to a supposed clash of civilisations was also demonstrated in the far south of Thailand where Muslim separatists are seen as resisting a pro-Western government. There are certainly cultural elements involved in a conflict which has been ongoing since 2004, but other issues are involved. Not only are the cultural factors more complex than the thesis of a clash of civilisation allows, including the problems of absorbing a largely Malay-speaking Muslim people annexed in 1902 by a Thai-speaking Buddhist state, but the 'cultural' issues are often actualised by issues of military brutality, which played a major role in the upsurge of tension in late 2004 in which troops fired on demonstrators, as well as by exploitation of potential conflicts by politicians and drug barons seeking their own local advantages.

Similarly, in Uzbekistan, the regime of Islom Karimov claimed that opposition was led by Muslim terrorists, a view that neglects the extent to which the dictatorship faces opposition for a number of reasons. In 2005, troops fired on a crowd in the Uzbek city of Andijan demonstrating against the poor economic situation. Yet, religion was a key lightning rod for tensions. In 2007, Pakistan forces stormed the Lal Masjid (Red Mosque), a centre of opposition by radical Muslim clergy, in the capital, Islamabad. In response, attacks on the security forces increased. The issues that led to violence might seem trivial, but the tensions were often serious, as in Kaduna in Nigeria in 2002 where Muslim anger about the planned staging of the Miss World competition in the federal capital, Abuja, led to riots in which many were killed.

Sectarian-linked disputes were not the only ones which were portrayed in terms of wider concerns, nor therefore the sole disputes to be internationalised. More widely, foreign assistance was sought, and, if necessary, hired to help resist insurrections. Thus, between 1993 and 2003, Ange-Félix Patassé, the President of the Central African Republic, survived seven coup attempts, including one in 2002 by General François Bozizé, one-time head of the army, that involved serious street fighting in the capital, Bangui. Patassé turned for support to Libya, which provided backing until 2002, and then to the Congolese Movement for the Liberation of Congo (MLC) rebel group, but, in March 2003, Bozizé, at the head of 1,000 men, overran Bangui. The unpaid army was unwilling to resist, and the MLC did not fight. Instability in the Central African Republic reflected the knock-on effects of war elsewhere, for conflict in Congo hit its trade links down the Congo river.

In West Africa, in 2002 and 2003, the Liberian government under Charles Taylor, whose seizure of power had originally owed much to backing from the Ivory Coast, supported rebels in the three neighbouring states – Sierra Leone, Guinea and the Ivory Coast – before being forced to step down in 2003. Guinea itself was linked to rebels against Taylor, the Liberians United for Reconciliation and Democracy – a misnamed group of thugs, as was the army of the Ivory Coast. France, in turn, intervened to support the government of the Ivory Coast against the MPCI (Mouvement Patriotique de Côte d'Ivoire; Ivory Coast Patriotic Movement): the rebel group that failed to seize power in 2002 but which remained strong in the largely Muslim north. Britain had earlier intervened in Sierra Leone in 2000, supporting UN stabilisation, retraining the army, and, in Operation Barras, rescuing hostages from the West Side Boys, one of the gangs that intimidated much of the country. Nigeria also played a role in helping maintain the peace in Sierra Leone.

In Congo, Kabila was assassinated in 2001, while, in 2004, his son and successor, Joseph, overcame an attempt by elements in the Presidential Special Guard to seize power by gaining control of state television and the presidential palace. This attempt was an aspect of the continuing role of force in the seizure and retention of power across parts of the Third World, a role that puts a focus on the attitude of paramilitary units alongside that of the armed forces. Military establishments have a disproportionate autonomy and impact in post-colonial systems where nothing else seems to work very well and where too many countervailing institutions have lost credibility and authority. Thus, in 1999, the Pakistani army staged a successful coup, although the military lost power in other states, for example in Thailand in 1992.

Coups and the possibility of such action continued to play a major role in military history. In 2000, American and Brazilian pressure on Paraguayan military leaders led them to thwart an attempted coup, and that year the army eventually suppressed an attempted coup on the Pacific island of Fiji. An attempted military coup in Chad failed in 2003. There were also military coups in Fiji and Thailand in 2006, although the Thai army was unable to sustain the political order it sought to create. In Fiji, the coups reflected ethnic conflict between the Indian and Fijian population. In Indonesia, the military did not return to centre-stage after the end of the Suharto regime. Instead, under the 'New Paradigm of the Political Role of the Military', advanced by General Wiranto in 1998, there was a standing back from direct involvement in politics. In his statement on Armed Forces Day in 1998 when he introduced the 'new paradigm', Wiranto stated that

> the Indonesian National Military would shift its role in politics and the national development process by not always being at the front of leadership, not to occupy but to influence, not in a direct way but indirectly, based on the willingness for political role-sharing with other national groups in Indonesia.[4]

The Turkish army proved readier to exercise influence against the Justice and Development Party, a moderately Islamicist movement, which won the elections in 2002 and was re-elected in the face of clear opposition from the generals. Yet, despite talk in 2008 of ex-generals being ready to talk about a coup, there was no action by the army.

In contrast, in Zimbabwe, in 2008, the military-dominated Joint Operations Command in effect gained control from the weakened Robert Mugabe and orchestrated the use of force in order to maintain him in power against popular pressure and democratic methods. The military, whose members and former members gained assets and government posts, was linked to violent gangs in brutalising opponents. Such violence interacted with economic problems in encouraging large numbers of refugees to flee to neighbouring states such as Botswana and Zambia but the economic competition they posed in a situation of high unemployment led to violence against refugees in South Africa.

The role of the military in politics is usually considered in terms of the Third World, but that may well underplay its importance elsewhere. If the threshold is that of tanks in the street, then there is scant sign of this role, but, nevertheless, it is relevant in three respects. First, and most obviously, the military plays a role in military policy that is often greater than the constitutional situation would allow, and with civilian oversight circumvented. Second, an ability to rely on the military is important in giving security to government as well as a capacity to implement particular policies. Third, the military may well have greater political influence in specific contexts. As an example, the military has had great influence in Israel in recent decades, not only with former generals playing a major role as politicians but also with the serving military being important in terms of policy such as settlements in the occupied territories and relations with other states. In some states, it is unclear how far the military is under the control of the government or how far it is in effect autonomous. This question is particularly the case in China, where the military appears far more autonomous than in Japan or India. The regional grounding of some Chinese units is also an aspect of the situation.

In the Third World, former members of the military were also important in democratic politics. This was particularly the case in Latin America. Thus, in 2002, Lucio Gutiérrez, a former colonel, was elected Ecuador's president, although this was not the happiest precedent as his attempt to pack the Supreme Court was declared unconstitutional and led to his replacement in 2005. Similarly, Hugo Chávez, who was elected President of Venezuela in 1998, had staged an unsuccessful coup in 1992 (for which he served two years in prison), and in office (re-elected in 2000 and 2006) betrayed a willingness to break with democratic norms. In Peru, another former military rebel, Ollanta Humala, a lieutenant colonel sacked for rebellion, stood for president in 2006, but he was defeated. Humala's candidacy was supported by Chávez.

In turn, in some countries, groups outside the military sought to use force to seize, or at least contest, power. Thus, in 2003, an organised criminal group linked to nationalists was responsible for the assassination of the Serbian Prime Minister, Zoran Đinđić; while, in 2004, mercenaries were involved in an unsuccessful plot to overthrow the dictatorial government of the oil-rich Equatorial Guinea, a plot that was allegedly backed by the former colonial power, Spain. Given the nature of the dictatorship, the only chance of overthrowing such regimes appeared to be through the use of force. Without suggesting any equivalence, military courts were frequently employed to support governments, as in Egypt where, in April 2008, they sentenced members of the Muslim Brotherhood to long prison sentences.

Alongside the use of force to gain and hold power at the centre, force was widely used against regional separatism. Thus, long-standing southern secessionism in Yemen, from what had been the independent state of South Yemen, was crushed in 1994, the Chinese suppressed Muslim separatism in Xinjiang in 1990 and 1997, while in 1998 the Tajik army suppressed a rebellion in the Khojand region of Tajikistan where many Uzbek speakers lived. In Nigeria, the army was used, so far without success, against tribal separatists in the oil-producing delta of the river Niger, the Movement for the Emancipation of the Niger Delta, which exploited the importance to Nigeria of oil production and responded to anger about the poor treatment of the delta region. In 1997, a separatist revolt was suppressed on Anjouan, one of the islands in the Comoros in the Indian Ocean. The breakdown in May 2003 of a five-month ceasefire in the Aceh region of Sumatra led the Indonesian army to announce that it would destroy the Gam separatist movement, in part by moving the local population into tented camps so as to deny them cover. This conflict, which had begun in 1976, opposed a military using the means of conventional warfare, including ground attack, aircraft, amphibious landings, parachutists and tanks, against a smaller guerrilla force lacking international support but strong in determination. After the tsunami disaster of December 2004, it proved possible to solve the crisis, in part because President Susilo Bambang Yudhoyono was able to sideline hardline elements within the military.

Supporting separatists from India in Kashmir, Pakistan, in turn, used harsh measures to oppose the Baluch Liberation Army, the separatist insurgents in Baluchistan who, according to the Pakistani army, are financed by India. There were large-scale arrests and 'disappearances', torture and the use of air attack on areas of Baluchistan deemed particularly dissident.

Conflict was more sustained in Sri Lanka, with civil war between the Liberation Tigers of Tamil Eelam and the government from 1983 until a ceasefire in 2002, and then the resumption of open military confrontation from 2006. This conflict, which has cost over 65,000 lives and imposed a formidable economic burden, drew heavily on Tamil separatism, which was opposed by most of the Sinhalese majority, although not all Tamils supported the Tigers. The latter relied on guerrilla operations in the Tamil heartland and terrorist strikes elsewhere. The government used its more extensive military resources, not least naval and air power, to contest the heartland, especially the Jaffna peninsula, but found it difficult to hold the initiative. The disruptive capacity of the Tamils was demonstrated in 2007 when they launched air attacks on the capital Colombo, using propeller-powered trainer planes. Nevertheless, most of the east had been cleared of separatist fighters by 2008.

In some cases of insurrection, separatism was not the issue. Thus, from 1996, Nepal faced a serious Maoist insurgency which posed major problems for its military, providing ample evidence of the difficulty of suppressing a determined insurrection. Helped by the mountainous and forested terrain, Chinese assistance and their own brutality, the guerrillas were able to avoid defeat and to continue attacking, which ensured that they remained a factor in politics. In 2006, having seized absolute power the previous year, the autocratic ruler, King Gyanendra, lost control in the face of street protests, and in April 2008, the Maoists won the position of leading party in an election (the monarchy had been provisionally abolished in December 2007). This outcome led to a coalition government in which the Maoists played a leading role and created the problem of merging army and guerrillas in a reconstituted defence force. The future stability of Nepal is unclear, and this may become a serious issue in Indo-Chinese relations.

The struggle between Fatah and Hamas in Palestine, a struggle that came to a head in June 2007, was not separatist in origin, as each wished to rule the entire authority; but it became separatist in character because Hamas ended up successful in Gaza and Fatah on the West Bank. Nevertheless, conflict between the two movements continued, notably in Gaza in 2008.

Sales of arms continue to provide fresh munitions for Third World forces, and their governments, encouraged by international competition as well as by concern over domestic stability, have been only too willing to spend money on the military. In 2002, African states alone spent about 14 billion dollars on defence. Expenditure on arms by terrorist movements was restricted by measures, including attempts to restrict money laundering, but, despite the efforts of aid donors, no such restraint affected states. Instead, developments in their military capability resulted, more minimally, from attempts to control the trade in weaponry and its components, in particular restricting the sale of components for weapons of mass destruction. Despite the terrible poverty of much of their populations, India pushed up defence spending by 14 per cent in 1999 alone, and Pakistan by 8.5 per cent, to total allocations of 9.9 billion dollars and 3.3 billion dollars respectively. Moreover, Pakistan's nuclear-weaponry programme may have been funded by Saudi Arabia, as well as by the sale of weapons technology, to North Korea, Iraq, Iran, Libya and, probably, Egypt and Syria. The key figure, the scientist Abdul Qadeer Khan, who ran an international nuclear smuggling ring, was disavowed by the Pakistani government, but in a scarcely convincing fashion. As India also developed an atomic capability, Pakistan was unable to achieve a competitive edge that would permit it to cut defence expenditure.[5]

Rivalry over Kashmir between India and Pakistan led to the Kargil conflict in 1999 (see pp. 44–5) and took them close to war in 2002, with the Indians moving over 600,000 troops to the frontier. Religious hatred between Muslim Pakistan and Hindu-dominated India exacerbated national rivalry which was made more serious by their increased nuclear capability, which led first India and then Pakistan to test nuclear weapons in 1998. That year, moreover, Pakistan test-fired its new Ghauri intermediate-range missile, while India fired its new long-range Agni 2 missile the following year. Its range is 2,000–3,000 kilometres, extending to Tehran, the capital of Iran, and covering most of China and South-East Asia. In 2003, both states test-fired short-range surface-to-surface missiles that could have been used to carry nuclear warheads. The Pakistanis have also fitted their F-16 fighters to be able to deliver atomic bombs.

These and other weapon programmes were designed to provide regimes with the ability to counter the military superiority or plans of other states. Thus, North Korea, which appears to have provided Pakistan with the technology for its Ghauri missiles, saw atomic weaponry as a counter to American power. Pakistan provided relevant information. In 2005, North Korea claimed to possess nuclear weaponry in a tunnel at P'unggye-yok. This was a clear defiance of any idea of non-proliferation, and one that was made more serious by the difficulty in obtaining information on North Korean capability and intentions.[6]

In July 2006, North Korea staged long-range missile tests and, in October 2006, tested a nuclear weapon. Meanwhile, Syria sought to develop chemical and biological weapons in response to Israeli conventional military superiority. On 6 September 2007, the Israeli air force attacked a military construction site in Syria. Rumoured to be a location for a nuclear programme drawing on North Korean technology, this site may, instead, have been linked to other dangerous weapons capabilities. The Israelis, in turn, built up a substantial stockpile of nuclear bombs, in part in response to the chemical weapons of its Arab neighbours. The Iraqi nuclear programme was delayed by the Israeli destruction of the reactor at Osirak in 1981, a bold and brilliantly executed air attack, and was definitively ended by the overthrow of Saddam Hussein in 2003, while, later that year, Libya abandoned its own programme. Moreover, in February 2007, North Korea agreed to close its nuclear plants and to permit international verification, in return for aid. On 27 June 2008, in an important symbolic gesture, it demolished its Yongbyon cooling tower.

Iran, however, proved unwilling to follow suit even after its violations of nuclear safeguards on nuclear proliferation were exposed in 2002 with the revelation of secret nuclear facilities at Arak and Natanz. Having suspended uranium enrichment, a more radical Iranian government resumed it in August 2005 and subsequently ignored UN Security Council resolutions that it suspend anew. Iran pushed on with work on a cone for its Shahab-3 missiles designed to ensure that the cone can carry a nuclear warhead. Concern about Iranian moves led to Israeli plans for action. These, however, faced practical problems (distance, refuelling, extent of reliable information), as well as the difficulties posed by Iran's ability to restart operations and the likelihood that an attack would unite domestic support behind the Iranian government (such support is a goal of the nuclear programme) and lead to a measure of international backing for Iran. The likelihood of Iranian reprisals in Afghanistan, Iraq and the Persian Gulf were less a matter of concern for Israel and, instead, offered the encouragement that they might lessen support for Iran as well as binding Israel and the USA closer together.

Weapons were not only purchased by states. They were also freely available across much of the Third World, which directly contributed to disorder and civil conflict. In the spring of 2004, hand grenades could be bought in the market in Mogadishu, Somalia for 10 dollars and howitzers for 20,000 dollars. These prices reflected plentiful supply and not limited demand.

The overwhelming majority of states in the world were neither leading military powers nor 'rogue states'. In many countries, especially, but not only, in Africa and Latin America, the prime purpose of the military was internal control, although its position was rivalled by paramilitary forces. For example, the Iranian Revolutionary Guard Corps, established as a result of the Iranian Revolution of 1979, was by 2000 better equipped than the Iranian regular army, as well as more important politically and more radical and dangerous in international relations. In territorial terms, the military challenge in many states comes not so much from foreign powers as from domestic regional opposition to states, some of it separatist in character, or from resistance that has a social dimension, such as peasant risings. The resulting warfare, most of which takes a guerrilla or terrorist character on the part of the rebels, is asymmetrical.

This warfare can also overlap considerably with struggles against crime, specifically wars on drugs. Thus, in Mexico in the early 2000s, the army was used against the powerful drugs gangs, while a paramilitary Federal Investigations Agency was established to the same end. The firepower used by both sides was considerable. In Colombia, the left-wing FARC (Fuerzas Armadas Revolucionarias de Colombia; Revolutionary Armed Forces of Colombia) guerrillas and the right-wing AUC (Autodefensas Unidas de Colombia; United Self-Defence Forces of Colombia) paramilitaries were both involved heavily in drugs, and this ensured that their operations were often designed to ensure control over drug-producing areas. In June 2004, the two groups clashed over control of the department of North Santander, an area on the Venezuelan border important for the export of drugs and the import of arms. The relationship between these groups and organised crime was close, but FARC also had a clear politico-military agenda, in which force was applied to pursue political goals. In 2002, FARC was able to put pressure on the capital, Bogotá, firing rockets at the presidential palace during the swearing-in of the President (it missed and killed nineteen in a working-class district); but the American (and British)-backed military was then able to drive it back into distant mountain and jungle regions.

Concern about both drugs and radicalism led the USA to provide aid to Colombia: over 4 billion dollars in 2000–6, much to the army, with an annual level in 2006 of 600 million dollars. As an instance, however, of the problems posed by drug wealth, some of the army units, in Colombia and elsewhere, intended to fight drug-trafficking were, in turn, linked to that drug traffic and its massive profits. In Colombia, helicopter-borne mobility proved a key advantage for the military in operating in the difficult terrain. This mobility helped in the recovery of the initiative from FARC. In addition, the political context was important. The government signed a peace agreement with the AUC in 2003 which led to its demobilisation. Similar progress appears to be the case with the National Liberation Army, FARC's rival on the Left. Nevertheless, the disruption caused by warfare led to about 3 million refugees within Colombia.

There are also problems with drug-related violence elsewhere, for example in Myanmar (Burma) and Afghanistan. In the latter, the War on Terror intersects with heroin production and trafficking, as well as religion and warlordism. The problem of drug-financed armed force is a matter, however, not simply of supply in poor countries but also of demand in rich ones. Indeed, the American 'War on Drugs' contributes to the profits of the trade, which is handled by criminal gangs that in part are able to force or buy protection from government regulation. The term 'War on Drugs' highlights the cultural tendency to view problems through the lenses of conflict.

The porous and contested definition of war suggested by its current usage, as in 'War on Drugs' or 'War on Terror', further complicates understandings of force and legitimacy and makes it difficult to define the military. If the War on Terror is crucial, then the Saudi security forces carrying out armed raids against al-Qaeda suspects in which people are killed, or the Indian Border Security Force resisting the United Liberation Front of Asom in

Assam, are as much part of the military as conventional armed forces. Similarly, troops are employed for policing duties, as in Quetta in Pakistan in March 2004 to restore order after a riot following a terrorist attack on a Shia procession.

Crime also overlaps with social tension if not 'class warfare' as in kidnapping, practised, for example, in Mexico in order to raise money but also associated with hatred of the better-off. In 2003, almost half the world's kidnapping occurred in Latin America, and, with about 4,000 a year in Colombia and 3,000 a year in Mexico, they represented a formidable strain on society in total terms. Colombia considered it progress when the murder rate fell in 2003, but in January and February 2004 combined there were still 3,290 officially recorded murders there. The small state of El Salvador had 3,761 murders in 2005 according to Amnesty International. The following year, the Brazilian murder rate was 23.8 per 100,000, although this had fallen in cities such as São Paulo.

Widespread ownership of weaponry complicates these and other problems. By 2003, there were estimated to be more than three guns for every Yemeni, and the ability of the government to control the country was limited. This problem made the al-Qaeda presence in Yemen more serious and, more generally, contributed to Yemeni resistance to the government. In 2004, the army launched an operation in the north of Yemen against Sheikh Hussein Badreddin al-Houthi, a Muslim preacher leading a rebellion.

Similarly, in Haiti, large-scale ownership of guns exacerbated problems stemming from mass unemployment and poverty and a powerful drugs and drug-smuggling culture, and this gunownership challenged the country's political stability, leading to a major role for street gangs or *chimeras*. In Brazil, criminal groups were able to challenge public order, though not governmental stability at the federal level. Thus, in May 2006, the PCC (Primeiro Comando da Capital; First Capital Command) attacked São Paulo, killing policemen and firebombing busses and banks, and producing chaos. This chaos led to a police response which was equally forceful. One hundred and fifty people were killed in the crisis.

The high rate of gun ownership in Iraq posed a serious problem with the overthrow of the regime in 2003. Alongside political opposition from insurgents in Iraq came large-scale property crime, as well as activity by well-armed criminal gangs, especially smugglers trying to profit from new circumstances. In Lebanon, where there is also large-scale gun-ownership, the autonomous nature of the Palestinian camps is one of the many problems confronting the government. In 2007, the Fatah al-Islam militants in the Nahr al-Bared camp outside Tripoli were able to mount deadly resistance to the army for nearly four months.

As an instance of military action in a different context, in June 2007 the Kenyan army launched an operation in the Mathare slum area of Kenya, a step directed against the Mungiki, a gang that ran the area and violently resisted police activity. Similarly, the army has been used in Jamaica against gangs. The Kenyan army is also deployed against cattle-rustling on the Somali frontier, a deployment that is of value to the USA which is concerned about al-Qaeda operations based in neighbouring Somalia, the classic failed state. In early 2007, concern about Islamist forces escaping from Somalia led the Kenyan army to move up to the frontier.

The challenge to states from domestic opposition is internationalised in so far as there may be foreign support for such opposition, or international humanitarian concern about the issue, as in Zimbabwe where the army has acted as a brutal adjunct of the corrupt Mugabe regime. On the whole, however, the nature of conflict reflects an important aspect of international relations; namely the extent to which the use of force within sovereign areas (i.e. states) is generally accepted by many other states.

This practice of force is seen as a challenge to humanitarian interventionist precepts, but the latter usually lack military capability unless they conform with the goals of great-power diplomacy. A more typical instance of intervention is that in Uganda. The brutal rebellion by the Lord's Resistance Army in the north of the country was backed by the Muslim government in Sudan in response to Ugandan government support for the rebels in southern Sudan. Similar patterns of activity have occurred in the past decade in West Africa, linking Guinea, Sierra Leone and Ivory Coast, as well as also centring on Congo. In Uganda, the rebels targeted children for abduction as fighters or sex slaves, and the rebellion had by 2004 led about 95 per cent of the region's population, over 1.5 million people, to flee.

In this and other conflicts, aside from deaths due to slaughter, there was also the destruction of the economy, as military units focused on plundering villages. Moreover, the infrastructure collapsed, with resulting deaths from privation as well as from disease. In part, the latter reflected disruption, for example to water supplies, but the spread of disease by both troops and refugees was also important. In Africa, refugees spread malaria. The Angolan civil war led to over 3 million people being displaced.

Such instability is particularly savage in Africa and the Middle East but is not restricted to them. For example, the situation in Oceania, the islands of the Pacific, became more unstable as imperial presences receded. Internal disputes over jobs and other opportunities were exacerbated by economic problems, and the resulting disagreements led to a high level of tension in which violence became common and sapped any sense of security. The results were endemic strife, and armed gangs of unemployed youths challenge the social order in Papua New Guinea. In the Solomon Islands, serious ethnic conflicts led to a coup in 2000, the year in which there was also an attempted coup in Fiji which included a bloody, but unsuccessful, army mutiny. In 2006, rioting and conflict between police and army led to a collapse of security in East Timor, while a coup occurred in Fiji. Paradoxically, this disorder led former imperial powers to send troops and police back into the region. In 2006, Australian and New Zealand troops and police were sent into East Timor, the Solomon Islands and Tonga to try to preserve civil order.

The overlap between political disorder and civil conflict was also seen in South Asia. Thus, in Bangladesh, the two main political parties, the Bangladesh Nationalist Party and the Awami League, compete violently as well as electorally, with mob violence, strikes, targeted assassinations and politicised judicial decisions all part of the processes. Weapons, especially staves, are used in street battles, while politicians wear bullet-proof vests. Such a level of violence threatens to effect a transition, from what can be seen as politics by other means, to a subversion of politics, as in 2004 when the leader of the Bangladesh opposition was nearly killed by a grenade attack at an election rally. The military feels itself obliged to try to contain the political violence. In India, there was religious violence in 2002, especially attacks on Muslims in Gujarat.

The overlap of such disorder with international tensions is widespread. In the case of India, bomb blasts in Mumbai were seen as a response to the Gujarat violence and were blamed on Muslim extremists based in Pakistan. In Turkey, external intervention played a key role, with Kurdish insurgents operating from bases in northern Iraq. In turn, this action led to incursions by Turkish forces into Iraq, as in 2008. These incursions reflected the degree to which Turkish nationalism is directed against the Kurds: the Turkish army sees its role in part as the resister of Kurdish aspirations.

In part, such conflicts also arise from the nature of international frontiers and their interaction with rival states, ideologies and nationalisms. While it is a commonplace to blame the legacy of Western imperialism for this situation, this blame frequently presumes the alternative of a clear border that, in practice, is generally far from the case. At any rate, frontier disputes remain part of the agenda of international relations and frequently, such as that between Thailand and Cambodia in 2008, lead to military confrontations or, as between Ethiopia and Eritrea in 1998–2000, conflict.

The interaction between civil violence and external intervention provides a way to consider not only conflict across the Third World but also those specific conflicts in which Western powers have committed troops; in short, it diminishes the difference and contextualises the latter. At the same time, this comparison poses a difficulty for Western intervention as it indicates the extent to which civil conflict is frequent if not, in some countries, constant. Moreover, this approach questions the analysis that sees violence largely in terms of resistance to the Western powers. Instead, as in Afghanistan and Iraq (in the second of which the insurgents have particularly disparate goals), it is appropriate to note the high levels of civil violence. Moreover, this violence cannot be readily contained in the terms of Western intervention or by means of the attrition of killing insurgents.

CHAPTER 6

INTO THE FUTURE I:
THE RIVALRY OF MAJOR POWERS?

An understanding of the diversity of future wars helps explain the range of future conflict. There will be no one type of war, and thus no one way of waging or winning war. Military goals will vary greatly, as will political contexts, and the two are closely linked. Yet the linkage is also uncertain because there is a degree of autonomy: while war may be the pursuit of politics, the institutions for, and demands of, conflict have needs of their own that do not readily respond to political requirements.

Much of the assessment of future high-tech confrontation or war depends, at least in the short term, on two concepts: synergy (profitable combination) and information warfare. Both are seen as of importance to the rivalry of major powers, which indeed is the suppressed theme of the 2000s: at the same time that the War on Terror engaged the bulk of American attention, a deterioration of relations affecting China, India, Russia and the USA was of considerable importance. This deterioration led to public shows of friction, such as, in 2007–8, Russian opposition to American plans to extend the Ballistic Missile Defence shield to cover Eastern Europe, and to encourage Georgia and Ukraine to join NATO, as well as Russian withdrawal in 2007 from the Conventional Armed Forces in Europe Treaty. Hostilities between Georgia and Russia in August 2008 can very much be seen in this context.

The concept of synergy suggests that, in any future conflict, future success will hinge on the ability to achieve a successful combination of land, air and sea forces, which requires the development of new organisational structures, as well as careful training of commanders and units, and appropriate systems of command, control, communications and information appraisal and analysis. Advanced technology, and a sense that technology could, would, indeed must, continue to advance, and that this has to be planned for, greatly contributes to ideas of synergetical warfare, which reflect an awareness of the requirement for a more sophisticated command and planning environment and also a need to do more than simply respond to the possibilities created by new weapons. Instead of treating these factors in isolation, their impact is to be multiplied by careful cooperation within and outside of new organisational structures. Thus, for example, as has been discussed, if high-speed aircraft capable of 'skipping' on the upper atmosphere and of transporting troops anywhere in the world within two hours are developed, then their successful operational usage will depend, to a considerable extent, on such cooperation.

Given that most discussion of future war between major powers focuses on American, or, at least, Western forces, weaponry and doctrine, competing with those of autocratic governments, especially China and Russia,[1] it is worth noting that future war, or, at least, confrontation, could also be between China and India, or even China and Russia. Whereas, in the 1960s, either of the latter would have found the Chinese stronger on numbers than weapons, the situation is different now. Furthermore, in contrast to the emphasis in modern discussion on a lack of Western interest in territorial expansion, it is appropriate to note the role of frontier disputes and issues between China and both India and Russia. In the former case, dispute over the Himalayan frontier led to a short war in 1962 that was won by China. This victory makes China keen on the regional status quo, linking in to Chinese sensitivities over Tibet, and also relates to interest in frontier disputes between India and Pakistan and in keeping Nepal out of an Indian bloc.

In the case of Russia, there is also a Chinese grievance. Russia gained the Amur region in 1858 and the Ussuri region in 1860, a frontier delimited by the Treaty of Beijing of 1860, which was wrung from the Chinese in a year of defeat and humiliation: Beijing was occupied by Anglo-French forces that year. Although far from being at the forefront of strategic concerns at present, this is unfinished business, and the past Chinese concern to regain Hong

Kong and Macau is a reminder of sensitivity to these nineteenth-century losses. Regaining these territories, however, would undermine the Russian position in Siberia and provide opportunities for enhanced Chinese influence and resource sequestration, whether in cooperation with, or in opposition to, the Russians.

While such a conflict appears implausible in a world defined in terms of Western action, and the reaction to it, this prospectus of Sino-Russian conflict seems less implausible if the emphasis is on future resource competition, not least in order to meet the demanding needs of Chinese economic expansion. Indeed, the tensions of scarcity discussed in the next chapter may prove as potent in the case of major powers. Were a conflict to occur between China and Russia, it is likely to be waged without the concern to minimise civilian and military losses that characterises Western operations; although it would be unclear whether it would be possible to contain the conflict or whether nuclear weaponry would be employed. At the operational level, there is likely to be a similar emphasis on mobility to that in Western warfare but also a greater reliance on the attritional characteristics of firepower and a greater willingness to engage in frontal attacks (provided that there is a firepower advantage), rather than searching for a vulnerable flank as the Americans did in the Gulf wars.

The vulnerability of the Russian Far East to Chinese attack from Manchuria makes the situation very different to operating into Siberia. For the Chinese, an advance overland to the Sea of Okhotsk in order to cut off the region, followed by the capture of Vladivostok might appear a tempting 'small war', especially if Russian control of the Far East had already ceased to be effective or if the Russians were already heavily engaged in Central Asia and the Caucasus. The extent to which 'small wars' between nuclear powers have been made redundant by their weaponry has been challenged by the recent experience of sabre-rattling between India and Pakistan, and, rather than making such conflict redundant, it may keep it limited.

At present, a common concern about the USA helps ensure that Russia has relatively close relations with China, not least through the Shanghai Co-Operation Organization, which, in 2005 and 2007, held joint military manoeuvres: Peace Mission

2005 and Peace Mission 2007. The first appeared to be a practice for an amphibious attack on Taiwan. Yet, a Russia determined to retain its position in the Far East, needing to secure its Siberian resources and wary of Chinese–Islamic links, for example cooperation with Iran and Chinese interest in Central Asian resources, may come to see China as hostile, especially if America's role becomes less prominent. East of the Ural Mountains, the ratio of Chinese to Russians is 100 to 1, which will pose further challenges to stability in the region as competition for resources only worsens in the years to come.

On geo-strategic lines, Russian concern about China should encourage Russian cooperation with the USA, but such a relationship can easily be mishandled in an atmosphere of distrust and as a result of the search for national interest. Russian anger with defeat in the Cold War and concern over American globalist pretensions and particular policies, anger and concern amply demonstrated in 2007–8, have indeed led to an identification of the USA as a threat that has encouraged a positive Russian response to Chinese approaches, which has been clearly revealed by the large-scale arms sales to China that have helped keep the Russian arms industry buoyant. More generally, this industry has benefited from a revival in Russian military expenditure, with a major programme of investment announced in February 2007. The Russians have also profited from the end of the Cold War in that they are able to sell to former opponents elsewhere in the world. Moreover, the Russians, like the Chinese, lack the restraints stemming from humanitarian and ideological concerns that have restrained Western governments from approving sales.

In an echo of the dispute over responsibility for the appeasement of Nazi Germany by both the Western powers and the Soviet Union, a less than robust American response to Chinese intimidation of Taiwan may lead the Russians to feel that America cannot be trusted (it will also affect the Japanese), while concern about the position in the Russian Far East may also lead to a sense that it would be better for Russia if China and the USA clashed. In the event of such a clash, the USA has a number of strategic partners. For long, Japan was the key one, but the Bush years saw the pronounced strengthening of the strategic partnership with Australia and the creation of a new one with India. The latter was based on American support for Indian nuclear ambitions, a policy that breached agreements on nuclear non-proliferation, and, on the American side, was driven by concern about the need for allies. This need linked two American strategic concerns: China and the Islamic world.

Both Japan and India are major military powers, and each feels challenged by another state that is unpredictable and that may be supported by China: Pakistan and North Korea respectively. In 2007, the USA reaffirmed its commitment to protect Japan against both conventional and nuclear threats, a key shield against North Korea, as well as agreeing to give this commitment teeth by deploying anti-ballistic missile systems. Moreover, the Japanese economy and fiscal system will probably remain well integrated with that of the USA, and that of India will become more so as the state socialism of the past is abandoned. In 2005, India and the USA agreed a defence pact designed to improve cooperation, notably in weapons procurement. The same year, agreement was reached on cooperation in civil nuclear technology, an agreement preserved in 2008 when Indian internal politics threatened to derail it. The development of a new strategic partnership between India and the USA was a break with former tensions arising from India's interpretation of its non-aligned stance and American sanctions due to India's stance on nuclear weaponry. India's economic growth and rising self-confidence make it more attractive as a partner.

Yet, neither India nor Japan are comfortable in the role of ally against China. Both feel vulnerable to Chinese attack, and rightly so, and neither wishes to lose the degree of flexibility about policy that they currently possess. China is India's largest trading power, and India is looking for a growth in cooperation with China, not competition. Similarly, China has tried to get on with India, to that end separating its India policy from its Pakistan policy. China's priority is Taiwan, not the Indian Ocean. In addition, despite considerable investment in military modernisation, Indian and Japanese force structures and doctrines are not designed for an offensive war against China.

If, in the event of war between China and the USA, India and Japan simply protect their space against Chinese attack, that will be of only limited value to the Americans. The failure of the much-subsidised Pakistani and Turkish militaries to come to the support of the USA in the Gulf War of 1990–1, let alone in 2003, and the refusal of Turkey to permit use of its territory for operations against Iraq in 2003, are warnings about any reliance on India and Japan. For political reasons, these states are unlikely to take part in operations against China, and, indeed, in the event of such a war, the Indian military is likely to be most concerned about Pakistan. The Indian Left, which plays a prominent role in the alliance politics necessary to the formation of Indian governments, is opposed to a nuclear deal with the USA.

Other allies will probably be found wanting in any American clash with China, for states as varied as Australia, Israel, Canada and Germany are unlikely to meet the requirements of American policy. Indeed, past examples, such as the Vietnam War and the two Gulf wars, reveal a conditionality in support that is unwelcome to America; while, on the other hand, allies feel a lack of consultation and a concern about American policy-making processes. The problem of alliances involves not simply the tussle of interests but also serious issues of comprehension because, whatever the rhetoric of shared values, there are differences. These, however, become greatly magnified by the habit of extrapolating differences onto the background of two different states rather than understanding them, more appropriately in terms of the continuum of values present in most states and the accompanying differences and tension. The latter is certainly the case with the USA, but there is a habit (understandable and seen also elsewhere) of ignoring this tension and, instead, expecting allies to meet American governmental expectations.

Concern about consultation is fully understandable in political terms but poses difficulties for military planning in both the pre-conflict and conflict stages of any confrontation or war: both stages are now very high tempo, while alliance cooperation raises issues of security as well as speed, as was seen in the Kosovo War of 1999. Yet, the consequences of democratisation and popular politics are a demand for accountability in government that makes it difficult for states to accept the leadership of another or, indeed, the consequences of membership in an alliance. The notion that alliances may lead to unwelcome steps is antipathetical to the democratising principles and practices already referred to, which reflects the extent to which nationhood does not act as a building block for global cooperation but, rather, both as a delimitation of concern and a demand for independence. This situation is abundantly the case as far as trade is concerned but is also the case for military action.

From a different angle, globalism and worldwide commitments will continue to pose major problems of prioritisation for the West, which may encourage restraint or, alternatively, a resort to war in order to try to settle an issue. The multiplicity of problems and commitments facing Western powers will limit the ability to respond to fresh problems – an issue dramatised for the USA by the need to plan for 'two-front' commitments. This need may lead to the reliance on a rapid response in a particular crisis – the use of force in order to end the need to use force – which risks proving as unsuccessful in the future as it has often done in the past.

Chinese strategic culture has attracted considerable interest, not least the question of the degree of aggressiveness and expansionism involved.[2] The Chinese showed, with their intervention in Korea in 1950–3, their successful conflict with India in 1962 and their invasion of Vietnam in 1979, that they were determined to assert their power when it seemed both necessary and possible. Chinese prosperity has helped to make it more assertive, as has the sense of a need to return to an intrinsic great-power status which was compromised by the West in the nineteenth century. Russian weakness (whatever the aggression displayed in 2008) and the absence of a universalist Russian ideology comparable to the liberal global interventionism of the USA, have made it more likely that China's opponent in any great-power struggle will be the USA. This situation will also reflect America's specific interests in the West Pacific and, to a lesser extent, South-East Asia, as well as a more general American concern to preserve the international order that it has created.

In the case of Communist China, there is also a tradition of American hostility, alongside the search for better relations.

This tradition, and its location in terms of the political culture of the two states, provides both sides with a ready vocabulary for dispute. The 'comprehensive engagement' that America under President Clinton sought with China was designed to limit Chinese revisionism of the international order and included unsuccessful attempts to dissuade the Chinese from transferring advanced weaponry to hostile states. China had demonstrated its aggressiveness with the Taiwan Strait crisis of 1995–6, and, indeed, Taiwan has been described as the Alsace-Lorraine of the twenty-first century, in short as the cause of revisionism.[3] Under President George W. Bush, constructive engagement was constrained by greater American criticism of what were seen as hostile Chinese policies; although the wish to secure Chinese acceptance of American policy towards first Afghanistan and subsequently Iraq helped temper earlier tension which was dramatised with the Chinese downing of an American surveillance plane in 2001.

In 2000, the American government was warned that plans for a comprehensive missile defence system might lead the Chinese to increase dramatically their number of warheads in order to be able to overcome whatever system the Americans could deploy. To this end, China is seeking to upgrade its intercontinental ballistic missiles, making the missiles more mobile and the warheads more accurate. The entry of India and Pakistan into the ranks of the nuclear powers has made China's position look less secure and has increased the sensitivity of the issue of missile defence and deployment. Chinese interest in developing intermediate-range missile systems are, in part, a reply. Any increase in Chinese nuclear weaponry will lead to a response by India.

China's long-term Versailles complex – the sense that it has been wronged by history – remains powerful and needs to be considered when reassurance is offered about the intentions of the current generation of Communist leaders. The return of Hong Kong and Macau removed prime irritants in relations with the West, but foreign concern about human rights within China, especially those of religious groups and Tibetans, is seen as unacceptable, and this concern has greatly affected relations with the USA, a reminder that conventional 'realist' approaches to international relations have to be expanded to take note of ideological alignments and dynamics.

Furthermore, the very fact of American power in East Asia, let alone the ability of America to act to defend Taiwanese sovereignty, are unacceptable to Chinese policy-makers, and may become more so in the future. This parallel with French attitudes after the Congress of Vienna in 1814–15, and German revisionism after the Peace of Versailles of 1919, serves as a clear warning that the idea that the status quo should be the basis for future relations is inherently unacceptable to certain powers, as the status quo is perceived by them as both cause and symbol of mistreatment and international instability.

Revisionist powers are generally seen as rogue states when they seek to alter the situation by means outside those of peaceful negotiation; although, being realistic, such negotiation rarely serves the causes of revision, and to pretend otherwise would be complacent. As a consequence, revisionism is inherently a cause of instability, as is the response to it. Aside from revisionism, the role of traditional disputes, tensions and threats remains pertinent in East Asia, most obviously between China and Taiwan and China and Japan, in contrast to Europe where, outside the Balkans, they are contained within federal and collective entities.

Aside from differences in South-East and East Asia, and resource competition in Africa and the Middle East, it is possible that China and the USA will clash in the future, as a consequence of growing instability in the Pacific, where economic tensions in many of the island groups have exacerbated, and been accentuated by, ethnic tensions. In 2000 alone, this led to violent attempted coups in Fiji and the Solomon Islands. Since 1945, the Pacific has not been an international battlefield, as the defeat of Japan in the Second World War was followed by an American hegemony that was enhanced by the support of Australia and a rearmed Japan. A China with a stronger navy, however, may seek to challenge American interests.

This navy is certainly designed to be able to protect China's capacity to act against Taiwan, for example by ensuring a blockade in the Taiwan Straits or a defence against a Kosovo crisis-type strike on China mounted from oceanic directions. This concern is linked to the long-term maritime strategy outlined by Admiral Liu Huaqing in 1987. This strategy has been adjusted from one of peacetime building to one of war preparation, with more planning for joint operations. Chinese plans in this respect include not only amphibious campaigns and missile strikes but also submarine ambushes to restrict American access to crucial areas. The launching of major surface warships by China in the 2000s has been at more than twice the rate of the 1990s. Access-denial operations are seen by Chinese planners as crucial, for conflict over Taiwan, for any war with the USA, and for a role for the Chinese navy. The doctrine of sea denial provides the weaker navy with an opportunity to thwart the stronger (American) navy, and this entails asymmetric capabilities such as saturation missile strikes against carrier battle groups.

It is also possible that Chinese membership, alongside Japan, South Korea and ASEAN (the Association of South-East Asian Nations), in the ASEAN+3 network may temper Sino-US tensions, as many fellow members have close ties with the West. Yet, in the long term, if global economic tensions become more serious, this membership may also provide China with a degree of regional support. China indeed has been trying to persuade Asian powers such as Malaysia and Indonesia that their economic interests are best served by looking to it, rather than to the USA or Japan. Talk of Asian values has also become more pronounced in Singapore.

More generally, there is the question of the relationship between economic progress and peace, a question similar to that about whether democracies engage in war with each other. Although capitalism (like democracy) has been seen as a force for peace, capitalist powers have fought each other, as in the First World War, and, whatever their shared interests through trade, it is far from clear that a capitalist China will be a more welcome partner for a capitalist USA than Communist China was. Indeed, a free-market China may find it easier to capitalise on East Asian disquiet with Western economic policies and financial hegemony, disquiet that grew after the 1997–8 financial crisis, because the feeling that the West, through institutions such as the International Monetary Fund (rather than incompetent, if not corrupt, East Asian fiscal policies), was responsible for the crisis is deeply ingrained and has encouraged an East Asian search for economic autonomy.

American and European protectionism, limited economic growth, or both will accentuate these tensions. The notion of an effective Asian regional pact may appear incredible, but the European Union (EU) has shown that long-standing enemies, such as France and Germany, can readily cooperate. However, China's ability to act as a regional leader will be undermined by continued suspicion of its intentions, especially from Japan and South Korea, not to mention Taiwan. The Russian attack on Georgia in August 2008 served as a warning that major states would not necessarily be willing to see their interests thwarted. This warning was of particular note in East and South-East Asia. Nevertheless, Chinese relations with Taiwan improved in 2008. Moreover, in November 2007, a Chinese warship visited Japan, while in July 2008, for the first time since 1945, a Japanese naval vessel visited China.

Alongside the ASEAN dimension, China's membership in the Shanghai Co-Operation Organization, combined with its key role in seeking resources in Central Asia, has dramatically increased its influence in East Asia, understood in the widest terms. Moreover, there are important military, strategic, political and economic links between China and Myanmar. Such alliance links ensure that future confrontations and clashes between major powers would have a ripple effect. This effect can be seen in the Caucasus, with American links to Georgia and Azerbaijan countered by Russian links with Armenia (where troops, planes and air-defence units are based) and Russian support for secessionist regions of Georgia, support which led to conflict in August 2008.

Russo-American tensions have an impact in the Caucasus, as do American–Iranian counterparts. Iran has threatened to attack Georgia and Azerbaijan if they accept an American military presence. Tensions also move upwards, with the danger that regional disputes, such as that between Armenia and Azerbaijan over Nagorno-Karabakh (itself a disputed term for Karabakh), or between Armenia and Turkey, might draw in major powers.

There are Turkish military advisers with the armed forces of Azerbaijan, while the latter has turned to Ukraine for cooperation in procurement. The resulting rivalry helps destabilise the region, as well as encouraging further militarisation.

A conflict between the USA and China would test not only their military effectiveness, but also that of their allies. It is far from clear that such a conflict would be settled by a technological lead; although it is also worth noting that, while such a remark would generally be seen as a warning against the inevitability of American victory, the Chinese themselves have made major advances in their military capability, in part from borrowing American capability by trade, purchase and espionage. The relative ease of borrowing and development serves as a reminder of the difficulty of maintaining a lead in technology, provided the industrial infrastructure to permit production is present in both countries. Indeed, the continued spread of advanced engineering and electronics will ensure that in the future the Western dominance of advanced weaponry and the relevant control systems will be increasingly challenged.

Yet, in turn, American investment in research on such weaponry and systems is unmatched, and the nature of China's military-industrial base is such that recent expenditure on the military and on this base has not remedied their major weaknesses vis-à-vis the USA. The Chinese need to purchase advanced weaponry from Russia, which, so far, includes guided-missile destroyers, submarines and modern fighters, is an appropriate indicator, while the display of American conventional capability in conflicts from 1991 has indicated China's relative weakness. This impression encouraged a marked increase in expenditure on the military from the 1990s, a policy pushed under Jiang Zemin (President, 1993–2002) and his successor Hu Jintao. The sensitivity of military command was indicated by Jiang remaining Chairman of the Central Military Commission until 2004, when Hu succeeded him. This expenditure, designed to encourage modernisation, contrasted with lower expenditure in the 1960s–1980s.[4]

Chinese military plans include the acquisition of a carrier capability; but, as yet, there are no carriers, and, anyway, they will be unable to counter superior American carrier strength which, instead, is threatened by Chinese submarine development. In October 2007, a Chinese submarine was able to surface 8 kilometres (5 miles) from the American carrier USS *Kitty Hawk* and its battle group without apparently being detected prior to that. A different type of threat is indicated by the *Jin*-class nuclear ballistic missile submarines equipped with a Chinese 8,000-kilometre (4,970-mile) range nuclear ballistic missile. These developments mean that the USA needs to revitalise its anti-submarine warfare capability, which has been downgraded since the end of the Cold War. The Chinese have also challenged the US dominance of space by demonstrating an anti-satellite capability. Moreover, submarines, specifically the Class 094, of which six should be operable by the end of 2018, will give the Chinese a potent second-strike capability in any nuclear conflict. At a different level, Chinese naval forces were deployed to protect their territorial claims and oil interests in nearby waters. The key change is from a coastal navy to one capable of true blue-water policies.

The Chinese challenge is also apparent as an aspect of an increasingly far-flung Chinese defence system. For example, China's alliance with Iran threatens Western interests in the Middle East and South Asia, especially trade routes in and from the Persian Gulf. The provision of Chinese weaponry is part of the problem. Advanced C-series Chinese-supplied missiles make the Strait of Hormuz a choke point vulnerable to Iranian power, and this is exacerbated by the availability of Russian Kilo-class submarines as well as by Iran's mine-laying capability. With over half of the world's proven oil reserves in countries that adjoin the Persian Gulf (in order: Saudi Arabia, Iran, Iraq, Kuwait and the United Arab Emirates), and with these states more able to sustain production at current rates than others elsewhere (in order Iraq, Kuwait, United Arab Emirates, Iran and Saudi Arabia),[5] the security of this route is clearly foremost. Indian support for the USA is relevant in the Indian Ocean, not least as India may be able to block Chinese naval moves beyond the Strait of Malacca.

If advanced weaponry was used by the Americans in an all-out conflict with China, it is not clear whether it could fulfil objectives or survive a rapid depletion rate. As in the Vietnam War, the timetable of conflict by the two sides might be very different, and such that the short-term high-intensity use of advanced technology by the Americans achieves devastating results but without destroying the Chinese military system or overcoming the political determination to refuse American terms. In addition, recent experience, for example in the 1999 Kosovo campaign, suggests that 'just in time' procurement systems are inadequate, as they provide neither sufficient weaponry nor the sense of confidence in reserves that is necessary for operational choice and for planning. This inadequacy is a product of financial stringency and of a rate of technological change that discourages stockpiling. The difficulty of sustaining a conventional war might lead a clash between America and China to face parameters different in type but similar in some respects to those had there been a nuclear war.

The prospect of a nuclear war was, is, and will be, increased by nuclear proliferation. Were Iran to gain an atomic capability, then other regional powers would probably want one. If, indeed, Egypt, Saudi Arabia, Syria and Turkey joined Israel, Iran, Pakistan and India in having such a capability, then the possibility of avoiding nuclear confrontations might be remote. Similar points could be made about East and South-East Asia, an area of marked military build-up. The wealth gained by the Tiger economies and the oil states has helped to fuel the modernisation of their militaries, especially, but not only, in terms of procurement. The obsolescence of weapons systems purchased in the 1960s and 1970s has led to pressure for their replacement. This investment is largely in terms of conventional military power, with less interest in COIN doctrine and needs than at present in the West. Thus, Singapore constructed six new frigates, and India, in August 2007, invited bids for 126 medium-range multi-role combat aircraft, while Sudan, a very different type of state, spent much of its oil wealth on internal conflicts.

Economic growth and resource yields in short are recycled militarily. The resulting strength of regional powers then gives added edge to tensions, such as that between Iran and Saudi Arabia, as the latter seeks to resist what it sees as an ascendant Shia movement. To a considerable extent, the Western powers are manipulated by, as much as they manipulate, such tensions, and this dimension of the Iraq crisis repays consideration.

Looking to the future, it is difficult, despite the rise of private military companies, especially, but not only, in security and para-military roles,[6] most famously Blackwater, to see any abandonment of the notion of a specialist military. Indeed, the RMA, in this respect, is simply another stage in the move away from the notion and practice of the citizenry under arms. As a result of force cuts and of the abandonment of conscription in many states, there are several million fewer troops today than in 1989. Thus, the RMA is part of the search for continued military potency by societies that can no longer countenance the mass mobilisation and ideological and social militarism that characterised the conflict with totalitarian regimes in the Second World War and the first two decades of the Cold War.

To defeat Germany and Japan, and to forestall Communism, it had proved necessary to match the impressment and ideological coherence (at least over foreign policy) shown by these armed nations. Yet, both were inappropriate for Western social politics from the 1960s, let alone for the pattern of their economic development. As a consequence, the notion of the armed nation had to be reconceptualised, back towards professionalism, with the citizenry paying the bill through taxation. This shift not only matched political needs and military doctrine but also ensured that a diminished percentage of the population, the electorate, the taxpayers and the politicians, had seen military service and thus (on the whole) had been habituated to military assumptions.

A true military revolution, in the sense of an abrupt change, would be a return to the citizenry under arms, but such a return, although periodically suggested by non-specialist commentators, is definitely not necessary nor appropriate in terms of modern military technology. The equation varies by country: Iran, a state that has the ethos necessary for mass mobilisation, as it showed in its 1980–8 war with Iraq, is currently developing or purchasing and integrating specialised high-tech capability, such as missiles, submarines and atomic power. Nevertheless, the likely speed of a future major war is such that there would not be the time for combatants to move from specialised to mass forces; nor would there be sufficient advanced weaponry.

Thus, looking to the future, the language of total commitment will be employed to explain, justify and encourage economic direction, the retrenchment of consumption and the curtailing of civil liberties, rather than the mass mobilisation of potential combatants. As the Iraq crisis, however, suggested, this assessment may require supplementing because confrontations (as opposed to war) could be very lengthy, while the use of the military for policing units requires a higher density on the ground and thus more troops. The new version of the US army's *Field Manual 3–0,* released in February 2008, emphasised the need to understand post-conflict stability operations as an important role by making them equal with traditional priorities. The first task, in practice, overlaps greatly with the functions of other agencies of government in such a crisis, as well as of non-governmental organisations, but in a situation like Iraq there is an important military dimension to the task.

The Iraq War has placed severe strains on the US army, much of which has passed through Iraq, but not ones that are comparable with those experienced as a result of the Vietnam War. Instead, it is the strains placed on American public finances, and the very serious consequences these may have for future military procurement and activity, that may be more significant. However, these strains and consequences have to be considered within the context of the general fiscal policy of the Bush presidency, not least the reduction of taxation. An additional context is that of American economic developments, including an unprecedented trade gap and a crisis in the traditional industrial base. Thus, yet again, military capability has to be set in wider contexts, notably political, but also economic, social and cultural.

The specific character of American military culture and power is also pertinent. As far as challenges to authority within the USA itself are concerned, the government has a key ability to deploy, and preference for the deployment of, paramilitary units, the citizen National Guard, rather than the regular armed forces. Moreover, given the depoliticised nature of the latter, it is probable that the USA will be able to continue to regard internal violence as separate from war and, crucially, not part of the function of its military. This approach again captures American military exceptionalism and also helps to explain why the Americans underrate the infantryman. In practice, the latter is, at once, the most flexible tool of war and the prime point of contact between responses to external confrontation and to internal challenges. The general American attitude to the use of the military internally also conditions American ambivalence or hostility to the use of the military to maintain control and 'order' in other states, whether by America's allies, by its opponents, or by other powers. Iraq proved a challenge to this approach, not least forcing to the fore an emphasis on winning the peace.[7]

It is reasonable for a British author to ask where this all leaves Britain. In part, there is the question of whether Britain should indeed be included as a major power. Aside from what, at times, has seemed like a running down of the military, particularly the army, entailing major questions about capability, there are also serious questions about the strength and stability of the British state. These arise from a host of issues and problems, including relations between the parts of the United Kingdom (UK) and between the UK and the EU, as well as the legacy of the acute fiscal profligacy of the Labour government. There are also the more general problems of the sapping of effort and will, a sapping linked closely to the dependency culture and the sense of entitlement that government has fostered – not that New Labour invented either them or the assumption of cheap imports, and therefore higher living standards, which are characteristic of public attitudes. In many respects, the social policies of dependency and entitlement have been out of step with the active policy of international military engagement that the Labour governments of Tony Blair (1997–2007) and Gordon Brown (2007–) have followed, and this represents a fundamental issue of strategic conception.

A measure of this is money, although that is what money is: a measure of a more fundamental clash of values. The expenditure on greatly expanding the welfare state has limited the possibilities for greater expenditure elsewhere, including on the military. This is more generally true of Europe and, indeed, is an acute problem in Germany. In 2008, more specifically, reports indicated serious problems of obsolescence with the *matériel* of the French armed forces. This crisis encouraged President Sarkozy to issue a new defence policy in June 2008 intended to focus expenditure on high-spectrum equipment such as spy satellites and to do so by cutting the size of the army, from a current strength of 120,000 to an operational force of 88,000, as well as the number of bases, in France and overseas. The transformation envisaged for the French military includes a smaller presence in francophone Africa, but, in contrast, the development of a base in Abu Dhabi, the first base in what was not a former French colony. This base is seen as providing a more valuable presence than the uncertainties of a vulnerable aircraft carrier. Sarkozy's policy was met by bitter criticism, especially from within the military.

In practice, the transformation of the European militaries was less than that in the USA. European commentators might like to think that this made them better able to handle COIN warfare, but, whether or not that was the case, there was certainly less of a capacity for force projection. Investment in the military was lower in Europe, and it was only a relatively minor goal as far as the EU was concerned. There was also a fundamental difference between the European (modest) commitment to network-enabled capability and the American to network-centric warfare.[8] Whether the Georgia crisis of 2008 leads to a change in European preparedness is unclear. The pressures of domestic political presents will probably take precedence, not least as social assumptions clash with economic realities.

The more acute possibilities for Britain arise not from the issues of military transformation but rather from the extent to which Labour policies have qualified public support for defence at the same time as they have seriously challenged the notion of the national interest.[9] History occurs in the short term, and Labour's policies are a key issue at the moment, but the long-term legacy is also serious. Labour's policies will pose important problems when Tony Blair is as one with Shelley's Ozymandias, with the Millennium Dome being a prominent instance of 'that colossal wreck'. The mismatch seen with Labour between domestic commitment and external concerns is scarcely new but has become more serious with growing strains in the world economy, specifically relating to resource availability. Thus, many of the issues addressed in Chapters 3 and 5, and considered in the next chapter, are of direct significance to Britain, as they are to other leading powers. At the same time, it would be naive to suppose that Britain would not be greatly affected by confrontation between major powers or would-be major powers, whether, for example, China versus the USA or Russia putting pressure on NATO and the EU.

This possibility as much encourages investment in high-spectrum weaponry, such as advanced fighters and the nuclear deterrent, as does the activities and plans of rogue states. At the same time, it is all too easy to employ this argument in order to excuse military investment that may be inappropriate. The case of the two British super-carriers contracted in 2008 provide a good instance. The essential logic is political (Britain showing the flag) and institutional (a prominent navy) and, despite support from operational analysis and military-industrial policy, not military. Although the carriers are supposedly 'future proofed' for the next generation of unmanned planes, the increased sophistication of unmanned aircraft, such as the Reapers purchased from the USA and employed by the British over Afghanistan since 2007, raise questions about the practical need for manned aircraft, certainly as an ordnance-delivery system as opposed to, for example, for transporting troops. Moreover, although they will be difficult to sink, improvements in missiles underline the vulnerability of the projected carriers. In combination with threats from submarines and mines, it may well be the case that much of the navy will have to be used to protect the carriers, which suggests a degree of inflexibility built into protecting what will probably become an obsolescent technology.

Instead, it would be more useful to invest in a larger number of smaller ships that, in turn, could be replaced on a regular basis. These ships might also be able to address the serious challenge posed by piracy and its threat to world trade. While the navies of Singapore, Malaysia and (finally) Indonesia have helped reduce the problems in nearby waters since 2004, serious difficulties remain, notably in the South China Sea and off Nigeria and Somalia, which, in this respect, demonstrates the problems created by failed states. A United Nations Security Council Resolution in

2008 allowed naval forces to move into Somali waters. Somali pirates have attacked as far as 457 kilometres (247 nautical miles) from the coast. Insurance rates through the Gulf of Aden rose markedly. Returning to the carriers, in political-military terms, there is also the problem that British carriers will not be able to contribute much to the West in a sphere in which American capacity already provides an overwhelming advantage.

It has never been possible to invest for all eventualities, and defence planning has always involved the prioritisation of tasks and risks. This prioritisation requires a high level of skill and leadership on the part of military planners and governmental ministers and advisers, and the range of current and possible tasks has pushed this further to the fore. A firm sense of the national interest is an important part of the equation, but so also is an understanding of how best to define that in terms of practicality and how to prioritise the latter in terms of the national interest.

Turning to the more distant future, and considering technologies that are in early stages at the present, it is possible that different types of combatants will be created in the form of robots, cyborgs and clones. It is also possible that advances in knowledge of the brain and in genetic engineering may alter what can be expected from human warriors. Increased knowledge may also provide opportunities for action against combatants. At a different level, the possibility of using electro-magnetic pulses may be developed in order to provide tactical, operational and strategic capabilities. Some of the discussion of the long term may appear fantastical, but the world of robotics is already present to a degree in the form of automatic weapons that may be controlled from a distance, including weaponry on airplanes not under the control of a pilot. Moreover, it would be very surprising if there is no military application of advances in other fields, such as genetic engineering. Such developments might not alter the political paradigms of warfare, but they could certainly alter the conduct of war.

CHAPTER 7

INTO THE FUTURE II:
WEAK STATES AND 'SMALL WARS'?

Alongside the emphasis on reasons for conflict between major military powers comes the likelihood that most wars will continue to be different in character, with the themes discussed in Chapter 3 continuing to be pertinent. Looking to the future, there are structural changes in the world that suggest that more disputes will arise, while unless we understand the security agendas of the marginalised we eventually undermine our own security. The first structural change relates to population increase, which provides a Malthusian vista of conflict derived from numbers exceeding resources, while also, as in Algeria, Palestine and Rwanda, ensuring a large percentage of young men able to fuel conflict. And not only there. The speed with which armies were created in the 1990s in areas with new states such as the former Yugoslavia and the Caucasus was a testimony to the ability rapidly to give effect to bellicose plans. Moreover, once used to violence, it is extremely difficult, as the militias in Congo have shown, to reintegrate people into society. This is a pessimistic reflection as far as the future of Zimbabwe is concerned.

While it is true that birth rates in many countries are falling, and that aggregate global population growth is expected to fall after mid-century, it is nevertheless the case that the intervening growth is still seen as formidable. The 1999 UN Population Fund Study suggested a rise from 6 billion people in 1999 to 8.9 billion in 2050, figures that reflect not only the entry into fertility of current children but also improvements in public health and medical care that lead to a rise in average life expectancy, as well as the continuation in many countries of cultural restraints on restricting family sizes and on the use of contraception.

If the rise in population is one aspect of the modern Malthusian dilemma, another is provided by the extent and acceleration of climate change. This change is abundantly displayed by indicators such as melting glaciers, while climate change and population increases interact to produce such indicators as shrinking lakes, for example Lake Chad and the Aral Sea. Climate change will be massively asymmetrical in its consequences. These changes also have direct military consequences as they threaten individual and collective security. The melting of the Arctic ice cap is leading to new commitments in the Arctic, for example by Canada, as new trade routes and mining opportunities are opened up (and contested) and as Russia claims territory.

The rise in world population has tremendous resource implications, which will remain the case even if growth rates slacken, because, aside from the rise in overall demand for employment and resources, there will also be a continuation in the rise in per-capita demand. Indeed, belief in a likely fall in population-growth rates presupposes such a rise, as it asserts a virtuous linkage of economic growth and falling population. An alternative, predicated on rising levels of fatal diseases, is not anticipated, with the exception of AIDS (Acquired Immune Deficiency Syndrome) in parts of sub-Saharan Africa, although the disruption caused by such diseases may well be a challenge for armed forces in the future. This role would be somewhat ironic, as troops have been a prime means of transmission of HIV (Human Immunodeficiency Virus; the prelude to AIDS) in the region: the widespread conflicts of the 1990s and 2000s, particularly the intervention of a number of states in the civil war in Congo, ensured that the numerous rapes and the support for large-scale prostitution by which soldiers spread HIV were extensive in their geographical range. The devastation wrought by AIDS and the very different threats conjured up by the SARS (Severe Acute Respiratory Syndrome) outbreak are such that it is possible that research effort will be devoted in some states to ensuring that pandemics could be a source of political intimidation and military assault.

Across the world, rising per-capita demand is seen as function, both cause and consequence, of economic growth and development, but these themselves are a cause of instability, because, despite important and continuing technological improvements in productive efficiency (for example the quantity of water or fuel used in manufacturing processes), economic growth also places major demands upon available resources. In addition, irrespective of economic growth, demand rises because of important social shifts, for example the move of much of the world's population into urban areas, which will continue and which is linked to a decline in former patterns of deference and continuity, both within families and communities, and more generally. In urban areas, there is a stronger willingness to reject parental aspirations and living standards, a decline in self-sufficiency and an increased exposure to consumerist pressures.[1]

A particular problem posed by population growth and social change is that a high percentage of the population will be not only young but also male. Across the world, there is a disproportionate number of males born and surviving childhood, and this creates problems in terms of the poorly socialised nature of this young male population, not to say its excessive energy and repressed sexual drive. A heavily partisan interest in sport is one manifestation, but bellicosity can be another.

This point operates as a qualification of the commonplace argument that Japan and Europe are bound to decline due to their low birth rates, whereas India and the USA with their high birth rates will be able to achieve economic growth. Such growth may occur, but the availability of masses of young male labour may also pose a deleterious effect, due to the need to take them into the labour force in order to secure stability.

The problem of excessive young males is accentuated by selective abortion and infanticide problems affecting women, which is a particular issue in China and India. By 2030, it seems that there might be 20–30 million Chinese men without a chance of finding a bride due to the 'one child policy' and the abortion of millions of female foetuses thanks to ultrasound. This imbalance could have a powerfully destabilising influence. More generally, across the world there are about 100 million 'missing' women. In the Islamic world, the discrepancy between male and female numbers, as well as social and cultural hostility to assertiveness by women, helps fuel opposition to modernisation and Westernisation which are regarded as conducive to an unwelcome degree of female independence. Demographic pressures may also be affected by variations in ethnic growth rates within particular countries, for example Muslim Arab/Asian populations in Europe.

Demand for resources may lead to an abandonment of the general principle that frontiers are inviolable, a principle seen as a means to continued peace that is marked not only in the developed world but also in the Third World, especially in both Africa and Latin America. Instead, the search for energy and water may well encourage the seizure of territory between and within states, which will certainly trigger conflict. For example, anxiety over water availability may well accentuate disputes over both source areas and those through which rivers flow. Clashes between Turkey, Syria and Iraq over the Tigris and Euphrates basin, or between regional powers over the Jordan and the Nile, or in Kashmir over the Indus, are all possible. Population rises threaten water availability, although other factors also play a role, notably inappropriate farming regimes and inefficient irrigation systems.

Across the world in 2007 there was a global average of 8,900 cubic metres of water annually per capita, and that average is predicted to fall to 6,000 cubic metres by 2050. There are estimates that about 1.8 billion people will suffer from water insecurity by 2080 (with another 600 million facing acute malnutrition). The regional situation for water availability is very varied. Good in South America, it is especially bleak in the Middle East (where the figures are 1,200 and 600 cubic metres) and South Asia, putting great pressure on both fresh surface water and ground water.

The extent to which river flows cross international borders exacerbates the situation by making water allocations a key issue. Thus, Turkish plans to build dams on the Tigris and Euphrates and to divert water for use in Turkey are unacceptable to Iraq and Syria. In 1990, they threatened war when Turkey halted the flow of the Euphrates in retaliation for Syrian support for the Kurdish PKK (Partiya Karkerên Kurdistan; Kurdistan Workers' Party) insurgency group. In 1994, Sudanese plans to dam the Nile led to a reported Egyptian willingness to attack. Sensitivity over water supplies, much of which come from southern Malaya, leads to

Singaporean plans, in the event of conflict, for advances in order to seize these supplies. Water shortage, alongside hunger, is a key problem in Darfur.

Forests, and the land and resources they offer, provide another site of contest. For example, in 1999, para-military Chilean Special Forces police were deployed against Mapuche Indians who were in dispute with the powerful forestry industry. States will take a view on environmental issues not only because they seek resources themselves but also because they feel that environmental degradation elsewhere challenges their interests. Climate change indeed greatly increases the problems of water availability and management.[2]

For many across the world, violence is a better option than economic development or, indeed, as a case of the economics of plunder, seizure and expropriation, is a form of such development. More generally, demands for goods and opportunities will be a cause of dispute and instability in families, communities and countries. This instability will be accentuated because, by 2007, more than 80 per cent of the world's population live in countries where income differentials are increasing. Just as higher rates of unemployment tend to be linked to crime (although this can be cushioned by social welfare, and most of the unemployed are not criminous), so a sense of poverty, whether absolute or relative, encourages alienation and a feeling of violence, or at least the use of force, is a response, as with squatting on rural land, such as the Movimiento Sin Tierra in Bolivia in 2003. Across the world, about 2.6 million people live on less than a dollar a day. Rising demands for goods and opportunities will increase volatility in many states, and this will be particularly so in those that cannot ensure high growth rates and the widespread distribution of the benefits of growth, or that cannot dampen or control expectations. This situation is an additional reason why the global economic difficulties of 2008 are of particular concern, but, already in June 2007, the introduction of petrol rationing in Iran (which lacks the necessary refining capacity) led to riots. In 2008, food shortages and prices led to disturbances in over thirty states.

Conflict creates poverty, but poverty encourages conflict, including the oppression on which such economically incompetent regimes as North Korea and Zimbabwe rely. Endemic unemployment provides arms for hire. Just as damaging is the threat of decline into poverty and of the relative poverty which will be felt by those who are comparatively well off but who have not had their expectations realised, a group that may include sections of the military. In Manila, the attempted coup of 2003 in part rested on dissatisfaction among troops with their pay. More generally, the relationship seen since 1990 – of about 220,000 people killed in inter-state wars, compared to over 3.6 million dying as a result of conflict within states – is likely to continue. There are obviously problems with definitions and measurements; for example, how far should the violence in Iraq from 2004 on be classified as an aspect of the 2003 war, or how many people in Congo would have died of disease and malnutrition whether or not there had been war? Nevertheless, the trend is clear.

The spiral of economic weakness, social breakdown and political instability poses problems not only for states but also for companies seeking to operate in such countries. This situation is more generally significant because much of the world's raw-material production and reserves are located in unstable states. As a result, production and shipment facilities have to be protected, whether oil platforms off the Nigerian coast, oil pipelines in the Caucasus or copper mines in Bougainville. This need has led to a major rise in private military companies providing corporate stability. These companies play a crucial role protecting not only assets but also the transfer of capital flows for their clients.[3] Such private security is particularly important in Africa and is a fast-growing industry that benefits from a lack of regulation which is also very troubling.[4]

In many countries, economic growth may well not serve to assuage internal tensions, while there may well be no political or ideological cohesion within the state to encourage the elite to develop policies of sharing benefits or arranging welfare provision. As in the case of much of Latin America, the resulting tensions will interact with a hostility to the elite's modernising ideology and policies, leading to an internal dissatisfaction that might easily escalate into civil conflict. This conflict could take several forms, including violence against particular ethnic groups, but it will reflect the precariousness of government structures and the difficulty of developing systems of mutual benefit. In turn, the political and governmental challenge will be to try to ensure that struggles for benefit take place as non-violently as possible. This task will be one for all states but will also lead to more international peacekeeping missions with all the problems they entail for militaries who find themselves in long-term policing and garrison operations.

This schematic account, like the idea of 'war among people' as the pattern for future conflict, is more true for some parts of the world than for others.[5] By 1999, 95 per cent of the rise in the global population was occurring in 'developing countries', whose people often lacked adequate housing, sanitation and health services and were increasingly conscious of their relative deprivation. This encouraged both migration and tension. Moreover, it was estimated in 1999 that nearly 1 billion people were illiterate, which again increases volatility. Furthermore, there was a political 'impoverishment' in that the means to press for significant change peacefully within the political system were often absent. This absence was an aspect of the problem of the failed state, a problem that was far more common than the conventional use of the term would suggest. Indeed, from this perspective, many states were failures, particularly, but not only, many of those in the Third World.

The resulting politics leads to grievances and clashes over resources, both of a conventional type, most obviously land and water, as in Kenya in the winter of 2007–8, and of a more 'modern' type, such as quotas in educational opportunities, housing and government jobs and the allocation of economic subsidies. The two can combine and can have varied regional and ethnic dimensions. Thus, Indian groups in Highland provinces of Ecuador can draw on regional and ethnic dynamics for opposition, as in 2006 when their protests led the government to impose a state of emergency.

Weak states and small wars are classically understood in terms of the non-Western world, but this approach needs to be reconceptualised as it is increasingly the case that weakness appears to be a characteristic of modern government and that this weakness can lead to a type or degree of conflict that can be referred to in terms of small wars. Tension approaching to confrontation or even conflict within countries may be seen as increasingly likely as governments find it more difficult to persuade dissenting groups not to turn to violent opposition. In France, the Arche exercises to prepare the military to cope with serious internal disaffection reflected governmental concerns about stability; the current emphasis in France is on autonomous EU military operations or 'civilian-military' intervention operations within NATO, but the military will be needed if the police prove unable to control large-scale civil disorder. Indeed, the problems that have occurred in the *bidonvilles* near Paris serve as a reminder that it is mistaken to think of large cities as posing a problem only in the Third World.

In theory, modern states are far better able to control and suppress discontent, as they have the capacity to create a surveillance society in which the government possesses considerable information about everyone. Furthermore, the nature of the modern salaried workforce and (through social security) non-workforce is such that most people cannot afford to break from this surveillance society. Aside from information, the security resources at the disposal of governments are impressive. Their internal control forces, whether military or police, have communications and command and control capabilities that are far greater than those enjoyed even thirty years ago.

Yet, aside from the argument that the increase in the number of states has itself led to weaknesses, both internal and in terms of more border and other foreign disputes,[6] there are also widespread crises in respect for government and a process of social atomisation that pose significant challenges. Potentially, this situation will be accentuated by the danger, within many countries, that the decline of a civic nationalism will be matched by the rise of sectarian enthusiasms. In some cases, these enthusiasts will be unwilling to accept the disciplines of democracy: subordination to majority opinions and mutual tolerance against the background of the rule of law.

Whatever their capacity for surveillance, it is unclear that states will be able to suppress the resulting violence, in part due to the difficulty of the tasks, and in part as a result of the serous constraints affecting their response. Thus, peacekeeping as a military task will interact with what has been seen as the breakdown, or at least reconceptualisation of the state. This situation is more serious because of the widespread distribution of firearms. In 2007, it was estimated that there were about 875 million firearms in the world, of which civilians own 650 million.

In part, this reconceptualism of the state is referred to in terms of post-modern, although that is not always a terribly helpful description. It is certainly the case that, in both strong and weak states, there are strong trans-national loyalties (not new) which have become more insistent as a result of technological change. People who live in networked societies can be acutely concerned about developments elsewhere, and this reduces the capacity of the vertically structured state to contain the aspirations of its people, let alone to direct them. In a sense, all modern states, whatever their character and form of government, are therefore weak or may have weakness thrust upon them,[7] which is an ironic counterpoint to emphasis on the technological enhancement of the military. The interplay between the two will be an important dimension to the future of war and should be far more central to the literature than is currently the case.

CHAPTER 8

CONCLUSIONS

The literature on recent, current and future warfare is dominated by the language of change and modernisation. As is the general pattern in modern culture, change and modernisation are equated with improvement. Relative performance or promise are defined according to these emphases, as are the conflicts seen as worthy of attention by scholars, and therefore, in a circular sense, as contributing to their analyses. Such an approach, however, begs the question of what is a modern, let alone a more modern, style of military operations? Leaving aside the argument that war is becoming less common, an argument that can be queried, Western commentators do not generally define as modern the operations of non-Western forces, whether current or recent, regulars or irregulars. These 'little wars', some of which are far from little, are slighted, although, in practice, conflicts such as those in Congo and Sri Lanka are as, if not more, typical of the circumstances of warfare around the world than the Iraq invasion of 2003. In June 2004, for example, Congo saw conflict in its borderlands and an attempted coup in the capital by elements of the Presidential Guard. Similarly, in August 2008 there was a coup in Mauritania.

The problems posed to regional peace by 'little wars' led to the deployment of international peacekeepers as a major military activity for many armies, although, again, they tended and tend to be slighted. In 2003 and 2004, the UN and the African Union agreed to deploy 53,000 troops as peacekeepers in Liberia, Sierra Leone, Congo, Ivory Coast and Burundi and on the Ethiopia–Eritrea frontier, although, in practice, the numbers deployed were fewer and mostly all from South Africa. The same problem of willingness to deploy troops, as opposed to promises, also occurred in the case of UN forces in Darfur. In July 2007, the UN authorised 26,000 troops, but, a year later, fewer than 1,000 had been provided. This lack of troops was despite the use of such military service to help sustain the cost of armies. Indeed, on one level, peacekeeping entailed developed countries paying for UN troops who were overwhelmingly from poorer states.

Considering most armies in the world since 1990, and also looking to the future, it is unclear that the central narrative and related analysis which has been dominant for so long, that focused on 'high tempo' symmetrical warfare, is appropriate. Instead, it is apparent that it is necessary to devote more attention not only to 'little wars' but also to issues such as COIN, not to mention civil control. It is also crucial to consider the world as it is, one in which the bulk of the population lives in cities, which will probably prove the prime sphere for land operations.[1] Yet, at the same time, as the discussion in Chapter 6 indicated, it may well be the case that interest in COIN has now been pushed too far in the West, as various agendas of great-power confrontation can be outlined which require different doctrine, capabilities and force structures. The Russian attack on Georgia in August 2008 highlighted this point.

In short, there is the customary danger of present needs crowding out future options. This process is particularly understandable given the extent to which these needs are posed in the shape of difficult crises and the problems posed by serious financial constraints. The net result is likely to be a more profound weakness when confronting a different military crisis in the future. Responsibility will lie not only with the priorities reflected by these constraints – a target of criticism by military commentators – but also with the military's frequent tendency to focus on the present and to fail to give sufficient weight to alternative challenges. Thus, in one light, this work is a call for more strategic thinking, by military and non-military alike.

Overall, any need for reconceptualisation suggests a multiple approach to military modernity and an emphasis on its diversity. Such an approach does not accord with technological triumphalism, nor indeed with the tendency of governments and militaries to overestimate their own ability to achieve success while underestimating the problems of transition to whatever is defined as modern. Technological triumphalism, whether or not expressed in terms of the RMA, provides a crucial aspect of this tendency.

A different perspective for relativism in the judgement of military developments is offered by the reflection that the standard models explaining how change occurs pretend to an inappropriate objectivity. The action–reaction and task–response models suggest that military effectiveness is, in large part, a matter of responding rapidly to events and to the needs set by ably defined goals; but this underplays the extent to which perception is integral to both. A similar problem is posed by the notion that the spread of the methods of a paradigm, or leading, power creates a cultural space, or region of similar activity and norms, in war-making and, indeed, bridges such spaces as this spread takes place.

In place of this notion, the emphasis should be on how the selective character of borrowing military ideas and practices, both within and between such regions, reflects the need to employ with care analytical terms such as 'modern' or 'Western' warfare as if they readily described an inherent reality or process of emulation and diffusion. The same is true of other terms such as 'Oriental' or 'non-Western' or 'Muslim'.

This emphasis on the need to employ analytical concepts with care is not the sole conceptual point of relevance. There is also the problem posed by the assumption that perfect rationality is possible in the selection of appropriate weaponry, tactics, strategy and doctrine. Such a point can be taken further by asking questions about the tendency to assume that confrontations, and therefore military tasks, are predictable, with corresponding consequences for doctrine, training and procurement.

Terrorism and resource struggles are two important instances of actual and possible unpredictabilities. The varied challenges they pose include the need for military reconfiguration from deterrence-orientated structures and doctrine to a response-orientated situation. This transformation could, and can, be seen as necessary both to advance the interests of individual states, such as Britain and the USA, and also, were it to be possible, to help sustain a world order based on cooperation and progress.

Yet, the transformation to more responsive and thus active forces and doctrines can also be seen as likely to ensure a high level of confrontation, if not conflict, not least because there is no agreement on the character and goals of such an order. The latter point challenges liberal attempts to create an order based on legal codes centred on human rights, as well as on more neo-realist interpretations focused on power.

There will be varied responses to the arguments in this book, but, whether supportive or critical, hopefully all will draw on the need for 'evidence-based' analysis. It is, of course, possible to test ideas through war-gaming, but history also provides a key frame of reference, not least because it offers a reminder about unpredictability in developments and results. Military history, of course, serves a variety of purposes, including institutional education, academic scholarship, popular interest, commercial opportunity and collective myth-making. All and each needs to be considered when the subject is evaluated, and to judge one by the standards of another is not necessarily helpful. Indeed, it can be positively misleading. The call to teach military history, which is a central conclusion to this book, might seem to shrink the options to the educational process. That is not, however, in practice the case, for the teaching of military history, understood in the widest sense, embraces the question of the nature and sustaining of civic militarism, and also, indeed, overlaps with the issue of commercial opportunity.

To approach the subject in another typology, one that draws heavily on the role and resonance of civic militarism, there is also the question of the point of reference. The question 'Why teach military history?' can be approached in the abstract, but it also depends on the country and society that is in the forefront. The issue is different, or, at least appears very different, in Sweden or Israel, Spain or Estonia, Ireland or South Korea. As a reminder of the variety of social contexts and needs, in many states, indeed, the teaching of military history is an aspect not simply of civic patriotism, a task that Victor Davis Hanson has chided many American academics for slighting,[2] but also of a wider social engagement that owes something to conscription. This engagement is seen, for example, in Finland, Israel, Singapore and Switzerland. In these cases, as also more generally, the teaching of military history not only fulfils pedagogic purposes but also helps in fostering the engagement of the civilian soldier, including the civilian reservist, a key element in conscription systems. Thus, morale, as widely conceived, plays a role in the reasons for teaching military history and also in the content and tone of the teaching.

Conscription can be unrelated to immediate threats, the case, for example, of Switzerland, but, usually, this is not the position, and the Russian attack on Georgia in 2008 will encourage a concern with self-defence in many states, not least because it demonstrated the weakness of collective security through international structures such as the UN, particularly (but not only) in the face of major powers. Thus, the teaching of military history, whether professional, educational or civic, is an aspect of a threat environment, and the assessment of value has to take note of this context. That, indeed, helps explain the role of military history in America's culture wars, as its downplaying is associated with a downplaying of the threat environment; and vice versa.

The prominence of the threat environment is also the case with societies, such as contemporary Iran and Myanmar, where the politics of paranoia are crucial to the mobilisation of enforced consent on behalf of the government. In some states, moreover, such as Turkey, Pakistan, Indonesia and, to a lesser extent, Brazil, the military presents itself as crucial to national integrity and identity. A functional element, moreover, is provided by the role of the military in providing employment and social mobility.

Considering these and other cases serve to underline the unusual, not to say eccentric, character of Western commitment in the discussion of military history and affairs, both to intellectual independence and to academic and educational detachment from public politics. Indeed, on the world level, the pressure of public politics on education will probably become more salient as China rises in relative importance, not least as an economic-political model, and not only for parts of Asia and Africa. This point underlines the need to appreciate the diversity of national cultures within which military affairs are considered, with the teaching of military history presented as an aspect of the politics of these cultures.

The teaching of military history in the USA, by far the world's leading military power, is currently a matter of controversy. This controversy is not least due to the widely repeated charge that this teaching is being downplayed by the 'politically correct'. Indeed, it is widely argued that they are preventing the appointment of military historians in American universities and marginalising the subject as a whole. Is this true? Does it matter? Is military history desirable, a 'politically correct' question? From the contrasting, 'non-politically correct', dimension, and the specific perspective of military change, not least technological change and the so-called RMA, is military history relevant? Does military history have a future?

The last is the key issue, both for the USA and more generally, but let us first address the question of whether the subject is being deliberately downplayed or discarded. Once one moves from the easy polemic of press discussion, it is possible to see this in two lights. On the one hand, the problems facing military history are not unique to the subject but are part of a wider issue that involves the range of subjects that were central to the teaching of history prior to the 1960s. Thus, this discussion is as much a question of constitutional history, of legal history, of diplomatic history, of ecclesiastical history and of high political history as of military history. Indeed, constitutional history and pre-1900 diplomatic history have fared considerably worse than military history, not least because they do not have the support offered by the military academies and by widespread public interest from outside higher education. Each of these ensures that military history is buoyant, whatever the situation in the universities. To a limited extent, professional interest in the law operates in a similar fashion.

The sense of a wider issue, of shifts in the nature and understanding of history which are also relevant to other sub-disciplines, is not one that most military historians (particularly those not in the universities) tend to grasp, as they generally have the tunnel vision common to most subject specialists. Nevertheless, this wider issue needs addressing, not least because of the extent to which this issue is an aspect of a more wholesale marginalisation of the longer-term continuity of American history. In part, this marginalisation reflects a jettisoning of a historical tradition that looks back towards colonial days, the struggle for independence and the early decades of the republic, a tradition sometimes inaccurately referred to as the 'dead white men' approach.

In its place has come an emphasis on more recent decades, especially the 1960s, and on social forces and movements, as the agents of change. The same process can be seen at work in Britain, although there, as in the USA, the new emphasis often fails to make sufficient allowance for other factors that have crucially moulded recent history including not only economic trends, fiscal policy and high politics but also the impact of war. Thus, for example, the Second World War had more of a consequence for twentieth-century American developments, and was more central to them, than Civil Rights; this was the case not simply as far as America's international position was concerned but also with reference to its development as both state and society. War had even more traumatic consequences for the internal development of France and Russia, Germany and Japan, China and South Africa.

An emphasis on social forces as the causes and agents of change can misleadingly make military history appear redundant or simply the expression of social developments. This, incidentally, is an approach that helps those on the Left who see 'peoples' warfare' as bound to prevail over regular, professional forces, an approach which is of limited validity but one that flourished during the period of so-called wars of national liberation and which was powerfully advanced in the USA by particular readings of the Vietnam War. The current terrorism/insurrection in Iraq is seen by some in the same light, but it is necessary to note, first, the military perspective: that insurrections do not necessarily succeed, as was shown, for example, in post-1945 Greece, the Philippines, Malaya, Kenya and Colombia; and, second, the political point that, by any standards, many of these movements were and are highly undesirable.

The relative diminution of military history thus reflects wider currents including those in both society and in historical scholarship. In the former case, it is pertinent to note the degree to which the individualism, hedonism and atomisation of society associated with both 1960s *and* post-1960s values sapped general adherence to collectivist solutions and commitments. Thus, conscription, and the accompanying mental attitudes and social patterns, no longer commanded support, and, in part, this point is highly relevant for the context of military history, at least compared to the 1950s.

In the case of historical scholarship, it is possible when discussing the relative decline of military history to point both to the rise of social history and cultural studies and to the influence on historical work of perspectives derived from other social sciences including anthropology and collective psychology. This process is not restricted to the USA, which indicates that locating the issue solely in terms of America's culture wars is inadequate. Instead, considering this relative decline requires a broader contextualisation which is alive to the interaction of American and international developments.

Turning more specifically to the history of war, there is a tension between military history as understood by many, but by no means all, of those who are interested in the subject and the history of war. For many, particularly, but not only, in the non-academic world, military history is the history of war, a subject that should be about fighting, about battles and campaigns, troops and weapons. This operational dimension is indeed important, and military history should not be demilitarised, but the operational dimension and the experience of combat do not constitute the complete subject. Indeed, part of the tension in the discussion of military history, not least among specialists, revolves not so much around its neglect but, instead, is in terms of how the subject is treated. Here, it is necessary to note differences among military historians. The operational historians and those who focus on battle, sometimes unfairly, but frequently all too accurately, referred to in terms of drum and trumpet history, are indeed neglected within the academic community, but those looking at wider dimensions, such as the staples of war and society, and war and the state, are generally assured of an audience there.

This situation is further the case because the 'history' in these cases is as much explored by sociologists, anthropologists and political scientists as by those seen more conventionally as historians. In part, therefore, the discussion of military history today is a case of tensions among military historians and about the character of such history. This debate is not always explicit but, in practice, exists in terms not simply of the content of the subject but also of the way in which topics are pursued and presented, as well as of the powerful issues of patronage and appointment and publication strategies. These latter issues are difficult to discuss but are none the less important for that. Indeed, this importance can lend a shadowboxing character to public debate, with vague remarks about general attitudes when, in practice, it is the views of a small number of individuals operating in particular institutions that are crucial and at issue. Those of publishers are also extremely important, because, if the major presses do not publish military history, then it seems to lack scholarly weight. This situation makes it far more difficult for academics in this field to obtain posts in leading universities; and there is no doubt that that is a factor in the politics and culture of appointments – not least because of the American habit of validating opinions and individuals by their labels, as if a book or person was necessarily better because published by, or appointed at, Yale than Oklahoma.

It is easier to probe questions about the appropriateness of the standard approach to military history, because this issue moves us from the more shadowy world of patronage. This standard approach is characterised by a fascination with technology, both definition of capability and an explanation of change, and by a focus on the Western way of war. The West dominates attention not simply because it is indeed important but because it is seen as setting global standards for effectiveness. This prospectus, however, is an aspect of a misleading tendency moreover to dismiss non-Western military history as primitive, a tendency that makes it more difficult to devise an appropriate doctrine for waging war with such powers, which is a key theme in this book.

These fundamental parameters of the subject are, in turn, linked to other issues. The fascination with technology and, more generally, with the material culture of war, contributes to a presentation of military history in terms of revolutionary developments in war-making, rather than of incrementalism, understood in general in terms of an evolutionary change based on trial and error. This preference is mistaken, as incrementalism is crucial, not least in terms of the response to allegedly revolutionary developments. The latter indeed have to be assessed, a response to them defined and the response embedded in terms of procurement and training. These responses to arguments of revolutionary developments in war-making involve what may be seen as cultural dimensions, and these dimensions repay attention in a subject that is frequently overly oriented towards battle, whether operational or in terms of the experience of war. A response open to cultural dimensions is also less overly determined, not least in terms of the habitual emphasis on the material aspects of war. More generally, such an analytical approach serves as a reminder that the subject is far from 'closed' or 'done'.

The treatment of war in universities can be mocked by focusing on some research topics which are indeed far removed from fighting, and, more seriously, by asking whether an emphasis on civilians, atrocities or the memorialisation of war, all three of which play a major role in the literature, has been pushed too far. These are relevant points, and some of the war and society literature and teaching indeed tells us far more about society than it does about war, and more about victims than about fighters, let alone fighting.

Nevertheless, in terms of conflict, it is also clear that victory is obtained when one of the sides is persuaded that it has lost, and this involves more than just fighting. The cultural dimension is also present in the shape of very different responses to loss and suffering. Current conflicts around the world serve as an abrupt reminder that victory and defeat, suffering and loss, have very different meanings in particular contexts, and success in such conflict, in part, depends on an accurate perception of these contrasts.

Far from being ignored, war also plays a crucial role in international-relations studies, not least those on the rise and fall of great powers. Again, there is scarcely any sense that military history is ignored from this perspective. The subject can, however, be treated in an overly reductionist fashion, as in the tendency to ascribe likely, if not inevitable, results to more powerful economies. This approach was seen in Paul Kennedy's influential *The*

Rise and Fall of the Great Powers: Economic Change and Military Conflict from 1500 to 2000 (1988), which encapsulated a widespread tendency.[3]

There is an undoubted lack of interest in most American universities in military history. This is particularly true of the Ivy League universities, in several of which the serious neglect of the subject contrasts pointedly with the impressive memorials to the many who lost their life in war, as with Yale and its powerful presentation of loss in the First World War. This lack of interest is also true of the University of California system. Furthermore, a number of universities which were noted for the subject have lost relevant posts or have become less dynamic. More generally, many of the best and the brightest students did not go to graduate school in the USA in the 1970s and 1980s, those who did rarely chose military history, and, of those, few chose American military history. This situation, of course, matters. Military history is a key element of military studies, and it is unsatisfactory that these are at best spottedly developed in the American education system. Understanding of the potential and problems of war is indeed overly limited.

As the study of war matters, so it is obviously desirable. The question is whether military history is relevant, as an aspect of this study, and if so, why, and thus how. This idea of relevance was strongly challenged, directly and indirectly, by the belief in the RMA (see pp. 6–9), which was employed within the American military to deny the value of military history. It was claimed that the RMA made military history redundant by moving warmaking forward, in a paradigm shift, to a new plane. Aside from the point that the RMA can be historicised by reference to other revolutions in military affairs, an approach on which there is a useful literature,[4] the claim that the RMA made history redundant clashes with other analyses.

Here, it is not so much the case of the analysis that there are unchanging realities in war, though that is the theme of a particular literature, as, rather, the argument that military history throws light on the variety of military trajectories in the world as different societies have responded in contrasting ways to the opportunities and problems of their situation. This approach can be taken further if the emphasis in military development is placed on changes in 'tasking', in short on the goals and functions of the military, rather than a focus on capability, in particular on weaponry, a major theme in this book. Understanding the contrasting rationales of militaries, and how they rest on different strategic cultures, is important because this provides a way to appreciate the military drives of opponents. This analysis is particularly important for the West as force projection has become so important since the close of the Cold War.

Military history thus has a direct value as an aspect of understanding strategic culture, which now is a key concept in military studies, with military history proving a crucial aspect in these studies. Military history is also important as the repository of experience and, thus, the background of training. Experience is particularly significant, because war, at the tactical, operational or strategic level, is about the management of risk, and experience helps define the understanding of risk. Furthermore, when two powers begin a war, each generally assumes that it can win, and at least one is wrong. History helps explain victory and defeat and also shows that the balance between them was frequently very narrow; although the military's expectation from history can be overly simplistic: they seem to want historians to indicate to them a range of alternatives and give them lucid explanations of outcomes. Nevertheless, historical 'lessons' can be valuable. At the tactical level, staff rides are a useful part of training, while historical operational exercises can indicate principles of manoeuvrist warfare, such as concentration and defeating opponents in detail (separately).

This presentation of past experience is a continuing process. For example, the need to make historical courses relevant can be seen with a stress on the history of joint warfare. Such operations, and associated doctrine, planning, command structures and procurement, became more important from the 1980s and, even more, 1990s, leading to a more integrated sense of military power, as well as to a questioning of former boundaries between tactical, operational and strategic perspectives and activities. The reconceptualisation of military power indicates the interplay of 'real world' experience in the reformulation of doctrine, a process that also alters the parameters of historical relevance. Thus, American interest in cooperating with local forces, seen in Afghanistan in 2001 (see pp. 59–60), led the Army Command and General Staff College Press to publish *Compound Warfare: That Fatal Knot* in 2002, a collection produced by its Combat Studies Institute on regulars and irregulars fighting in concert. The Preface declared, 'knowing how the dynamics of compound warfare have affected the outcome of past conflicts will better prepare us to meet both present crises and future challenges of a similar nature.'

Reference to history is also widespread elsewhere. For example, in December 2000, Alain Richard, the French Minister of Defence, declared 'the place of history is fundamental in the formation of officers, in order to illuminate their actions and their role in society.' In 1994, the French Ministry of Defence had been responsible for the foundation of a Centre d'Études d'Histoire de la Défense, based at Vincennes from 1995.

A more specific cause for historical debate was provided by the extent to which history was used to suggest a frame of reference for debating military options. Thus, before the Iraq War of 2003, there was much reference in Britain by critics of action to the 1956 invasion of Egypt, the Suez Crisis, and by supporters to the Munich Crisis of 1938. In this, as in many other cases, 'history' served as a box from which words and images could be pulled for citation. This practice was seen, moreover, as the frame of reference offered, by outside commentators (sometimes well informed and often not) for American military activities in Iraq from 2003 moved from being the rapid success of the Gulf War of 1991 to the intractable commitment of the Vietnam War. In turn, in August 2007, President George W. Bush cited the chaos in South-East Asia that followed American withdrawal from Vietnam in 1973 as a reason for continuing to persist in Iraq. Compared to this questionable, if not somewhat crude practice (although a speech is not the place for an informed debate), part of the value of military history is that it should offer the possibility of a more sophisticated usage of references, not least in terms of the public debate.

Claims that a historical perspective on war is irrelevant are misguided, although, as discussion of the RMA indicates, they reflect a powerful impulse within modern American military culture that draws on a wider practice in the West. Indeed, for at least a quarter-millennium, it has been customary to emphasise the importance of an approach, insight or development by stressing its novel character and consequences; and the search for them has been an important aspect of Western intellectual culture. This emphasis on innovation has had multiple advantages, and to argue that military history should abandon its focus on the new and revolutionary might seem counter-intuitive, especially if cutting-edge technology is regarded as the great force multiplier, as indeed is frequently the case.

Military realities, however, are both too complex and too dependent on previous experiences to make a focus simply on change, let alone revolutionary change, helpful. An emphasis on continuities captures the role of limitations, especially of Western tactical, operational and strategic military effectiveness with regard to non-Western environments; although, of course, continuity does not imply an absence of change. Such an understanding, of both continuity and change, underlines the crucial value of a historical approach. The argument of this book is that it has a lot to offer the current debate about Western military effectiveness and possibilities.

NOTES

PREFACE

1 For a summary, J. Black, *Rethinking Military History* (London, 2004).

2 J. Black, *The Age of Total War, 1860–1945* (Westport, Conn., 2006).

3 J. Lewis, *Changing Direction: British Military Planning for Post-War Strategic Defence, 1942–7* (2nd edn, London, 2002).

1   INTRODUCTION

1 J. Mueller, *Retreat from Doomsday: The Obsolescence of Major War* (New York, 1989); C. Kaysen, 'Is War Obsolete? A Review Essay', *International Security,* 14 (1990), pp. 42–69; R. L. O'Connell, *Ride of the Second Horseman: The Birth and Death of War* (New York, 1997); M. Mandelbaum, 'Is Major War Obsolete?' *Survival,* 40 (1998–9), pp. 20–38.

2   A CONVENTIONAL ACCOUNT, 1990–2000

1 R. R. Leonhard, *The Art of Maneuver: Maneuver-Warfare Theory and AirLand Battle* (Novato, Calif., 1991); L. Freedman, *The Revolution in Strategic Affairs* (Oxford, 1998).

2 C. Coker, *The Warrior Ethos: Military Culture and the War on Terror* (London, 2007).

3 B. M. Linn, *The Echo of Battle: The Army's War of War* (Cambridge, Mass., 2007).

4 J. R. Blaker, *Transforming Military Force: The Legacy of Arthur Cebrowski and Network-Centric Warfare* (Westport, Conn., 2007).

5 A. J. Bacevich, *The New American Militarism: How Americans Are Seduced by War* (Oxford, 2006).

6 F. Zakaria, *The Post-American World* (London, 2008).

7 J. J. McGrath, *Crossing the Line of Departure: Battle Command on the Move: A Historical Perspective* (Fort Leavenworth, Kans., 2006), p. 225.

8 J. Olsen, *John Warden and the Renaissance of American Air Power* (Dulles, Virg., 2007).

9   J. J. McGrath, *The Other End of the Spear: The Tooth-to-Tail Ratio in Modern Military Operations* (Fort Leavenworth, Kans., 2007), p. 42.

10   R. H. Scales, *Certain Victory: The US Army in the Gulf War* (Fort Leavenworth, Kans., 1993); R. W. Swain, *'Lucky War': Third Army in Desert Storm* (Fort Leavenworth, Kans., 1994); A. H. Cordesman and A. R. Wagner, *The Lessons of Modern War, Vol. IV: The Gulf War* (Boulder, Col., 1996); J. A. Olsen, *Strategic Air Power in Desert Storm* (London, 2003).

11   R. M. Connaughton, *Peacekeeping and Military Intervention* (Camberley, 1992).

12   A. J. Bacevich and E. Inbar (eds), *The Gulf War of 1991 Reconsidered* (London, 2003).

13   T. Ricks, *Fiasco: The American Military Adventure in Iraq* (New York, 2006), pp. 8–20.

14   T. Karcher, *Understanding the 'Victory Disease': From the Little Bighorn to Mogadishu and Beyond* (Fort Leavenworth, Kans., 2004), pp. 34, 40, 45.

15   K. Allard, *Somalia Operations: Lessons Learned* (Washington, DC, 1995); M. Bowden, *Black Hawk Down: A Story of Modern War* (New York, 1999).

16   B. Shacochis, *The Immaculate Invasion* (New York, 1999).

17   E. O'Ballance, *Wars in the Caucasus, 1990–95* (Basingstoke, 1996).

18   L. I. Polyakov, 'American Defense Transformation: A View from Ukraine', in C. C. Crane (ed.), *Transforming Defense* (Carlisle, Pa., 2001), p. 18.

19   J. Hughes, *Chechnya: From Nationalism to Jihad* (Philadelphia, Pa., 2007).

20   A. Raevsky, 'Russian Military Performance in Chechnya: An Initial Evaluation', *Journal of Slavic Military Studies,* 8 (1995), pp. 681–90.

21   A. Lieven, *Flaying the Bear: Chechnya and the Collapse of Russian Power* (New Haven, Conn., 1998); S. Knezys and R. Sedlickas, *The War on Chechnya* (College Station, Tex., 1999); S. Smith, *Allah's Mountains: The Battle for Chechnya* (2nd edn, London, 2001); R. Seely, *Russo-Chechen Conflict, 1800–2000: A Deadly Embrace* (London, 2001).

22   G. M. Hahn, *Russia's Islamic Threat* (New Haven, Conn., 2007).

23   L. Wright, *The Looming Tower: Al-Qaeda and the Road to 9/11* (London, 2006).

24 L. W. Grau and M. A. Gress (eds), *The Russian General Staff: The Soviet-Afghan War* (Lawrence, Kans., 2002).

25 C. S. King, 'The Siege of Sarajevo, 1992–95', in W. G. Robertson and L. A. Yates (eds), *Block by Block: The Challenges of Urban Operations* (Fort Leavenworth, Kans., 2003), pp. 235, 273.

26 M. A. Bucknam, *Responsibility of Command: How UN and NATO Commanders Influenced Airpower over Bosnia* (Montgomery, Ala., 2003).

27 J. Gow, 'After the Flood: Literature on the Context, Cause and Course of the Yugoslav War – Reflections and Refractions', *Slavonic and East European Review,* 85 (1997), pp. 446–84; S. L. Burg and P. S. Shoup, *The War in Bosnia-Herzegovina: Ethnic Conflict and International Intervention* (Armonk, NY, 1999); T. Ripley, *Operation Deliberate Force: The UN and Nato Campaign in Bosnia, 1995* (Lancaster, 1999); C. Shrader, *The Muslim-Croat Civil War in Central Bosnia: A Military History, 1992–94* (College Station, Tex., 2003); M. A. Hoare, *How Bosnia Armed* (London, 2004).

28 M. Melvin and S. Peach, 'Reaching for the End of the Rainbow: Command and the RMA', in G. Sheffield and G. Till (eds), *Challenges of High Command in the Twentieth Century* (Camberley, 1999), pp. 120–1.

29 R. C. Nation, *War in the Balkans, 1991–2002* (Carlisle, Pa., 2003); R. C. Phillips, *Bosnia-Herzegovina: The U.S. Army's Role in Peace Enforcement Operations, 1995–2004* (Washington, DC, no date).

30 I. H. Daalder and M. E. O'Hanlon, *Winning Ugly: NATO's War to Save Kosovo* (Washington, DC, 2000); T. Judah, *Kosovo: War and Revenge* (New Haven, Conn., 2000); L. Freedman, 'Victims and Victors: Reflections on the Kosovo War', *Review of International Studies,* 26 (2000), pp. 335–58; S. T. Hosmer, *The Conflict over Kosovo: Why Milosevic Decided to Settle When He Did* (Santa Monica, Calif., 2001); B. S. Lambeth, *NATO's Air War for Kosovo: A Strategic and Operational Assessment* (Santa Monica, Calif., 2001); A. J. Bacevich and E. A. Cohen (eds), *War Over Kosovo: Politics and Strategy in a Global Age* (New York, 2002).

31 P. Ashdown, *Swords and Ploughshares: Bringing Peace in the 21st Century* (London, 2001).

32 M. Laity, *Preventing War in Macedonia: Pre-Emptive Diplomacy for the 21st Century* (London, 2008), quote p. 9, Aračinovo, p. 24.

33 P. Kennedy, *The Rise and Fall of the Great Powers: Economic*

Change and Military Conflict from 1500 to 2000 (London, 1988).

34 O. Coté, 'The Trident and the Triad: Collecting the D-5 Dividend', *International Security,* 16 (1991), pp. 117–45.

35 *The Times,* 15 April 1996, p. 10.

36 W. M. Donnelly, *Transforming an Army at War: Designing the Modular Force, 1991–2005* (Washington, DC, 2007), pp. 19–25.

37 R. J. Reardon and J. A. Charlston, *From Transformation to Combat: The First Stryker Brigade at War* (Washington, DC, 2007), p. 70.

38 T. Weiner, *Legacy of Ashes: The History of the CIA* (London, 2007).

39 *Strategic Assessment 1999* (Washington, DC, 1999), pp. 9, 13.

40 P. J. Scheips, *The Role of Federal Military Forces in Domestic Disorders, 1945–92* (Washington, 2005), pp. 441–9.

3 SIGNS OF DIFFERENCE, 1990–2000

1 E. Karsh, 'Cold War, Post Cold War: Does It Make a Difference for the Middle East?' *Review of International Studies,* 23 (1997), pp. 271–91; O. Westad, *The Global Cold War: Third World Interventions and the Making of Our Times* (Cambridge, 2005).

2 V. P. Malik, *Kargil: From Surprise to Victory* (London, 2006).

3 A. Clayton, *Factions, Foreigners and Fantasies: The Civil War in Liberia* (Sandhurst, 1995) and *Frontiersmen: Warfare in Africa since 1950* (London, 1999); T. M. Ali and R. O. Matthews, *Civil Wars in Africa: Roots and Resolution* (Montreal, 1999).

4 R. Dallaire, *Shake Hands with the Devil: The Failure of Humanity in Rwanda* (New York, 2005).

5 L. H. Keeley, *War Before Civilization: The Myth of the Peaceful Savage* (Cambridge, Mass., 1995).

6 J. S. Ikpuk, *Militarisation of Politics and Neo-Colonialism: The Nigerian Experience* (London, 1995); J. Peters, *The Nigerian Military and the State* (London, 1997).

7 L. C. Sebastian, *Realpolitik Ideology: Indonesia's Use of Military Force* (Singapore, 2006).

8 A. Siddiqa, *Military Inc.: Inside Pakistan's Military Economy* (London, 2007).

4 THE WAR ON TERROR

1 Had the buildings been completely destroyed at once without any opportunities for evacuation, far more people, possibly 30,000 in total, would have been killed.

2   W. Maley, *The Afghanistan Wars* (2nd edn, Basingstoke, 2009).

3   A. H. Cordesman, *The Lessons of Afghanistan* (Washington, DC, 2002); C. Conetta, *Strange Victory: A Critical Appraisal of Operation Enduring Freedom and the Afghanistan War* (Cambridge, Mass., 2002).

4   D. M. Drew, 'U.S. Airpower Theory and the Insurgent Challenge: A Short Journey to Confusion', *Journal of Military History,* 62 (1998), pp. 809–32, esp. pp. 824, 829–30; C. Malkasian, *A History of Modern Wars of Attrition* (Westport, Conn., 2002), p. 205.

5   S. Biddle, *Afghanistan and the Future of Warfare: Implications for Army and Defense Policy* (Carlisle, Pa., 2002), summarised in S. Biddle, 'Afghanistan and the Future of Warfare', *Foreign Affairs,* 82, 2 (2003), pp. 31–46. For a different approach, S. D. Wrage (ed.), *Immaculate Warfare: Participants Reflect on the Air Campaigns over Kosovo, Afghanistan, and Iraq* (Westport, Conn., 2003).

6   R. W. Stewart, *Operation Enduring Freedom* (Washington, DC, 2003), pp. 38–9.

7   J. Keegan, 'How America Can Wreak Vengeance', *Daily Telegraph,* 14 September, 2001, p. 22. For a far better-considered response, M. Howard '"9/11" and After: A British View', *Naval War College Review,* 55, 4 (2002), pp. 12–13.

8   T. Dodge, 'Cake Walk, Coup or Urban Warfare: The Battle for Iraq', in T. Dodge and S. Simon (eds), *Iraq at the Crossroads: State and Society in the Shadow of Regime Change* (Oxford, 2003), pp. 59, 70–1.

9   W. Murray and R. H. Scales, *The Iraq War* (Cambridge, Mass., 2003).

10   M. Knights, *Cradle of Conflict: Iraq and the Birth of the Modern US Military* (Annapolis, Md., 2005).

11   W. S. Story, 'Politics, Generals, and Iraq', *Army History,* 68 (2008), p. 33.

12   M. Etherington, *Revolt on the Tigris: The Al-Sadr Uprising and the Governing of Iraq* (London, 2005).

13   J. E. Stiglitz and L. Bilmes, *The Three Trillion Dollar War: The True Cost of the Iraq Conflict* (London, 2008).

14   U. K. Singh, *The State, Democracy and Anti-Terror Laws in India* (New Delhi, 2007).

15   A. Cordesman, 'Preliminary "Lessons" of the Israeli-Hizbullah War', *Centre for Strategic and International Studies* (2006); M. van Creveld, 'Israel's Lebanese War: A Preliminary Assessment',

RUSI Journal, 151, October (2006), pp. 40–3.

16 R. Leenders, 'How the Rebel Regained His Cause: Hizbullah and the Sixth Arab-Israeli War', *MIT Electronic Journal of Middle East Studies,* 6 (2006).

17 A. F. Marrero, 'Hezbollah as a Non-State Actor in the Second Lebanon War: An Operational Analysis', in K. D. Gott and M. G. Brooks (eds), *Warfare in the Age of Non-State Actors: Implications for the US Army* (Fort Leavenworth, Kans., 2007).

18 R. Thornton, *Asymmetric Warfare: Threat and Response in the 21st Century* (London, 2007).

19 J. A. Nagl, *Learning to Eat Soup with a Knife: Counter-Insurgency Lessons from Malaya and Vietnam* (Chicago, Ill., 2005); D. Galula, *Counter-Insurgency Warfare: Theory and Practice* (Westport, Conn., 2006); D. Marston and C. Malkasian (eds), *Counterinsurgency in Modern Warfare* (London, 2008).

20 J. Record, *Beating Goliath: Why Insurgencies Win* (Dulles, Va., 2007).

21 J. J. McGrath, *Boots on the Ground: Troop Density in Contingency Operations* (Fort Leavenworth, Kans., 2006), pp. 147, 135.

22 P. Boisson, 'Punishment in Syahcow, Afghanistan, 25 July 2005', in W. G. Robertson (ed.), *In Contact! Case Studies from the Long War* (Fort Leavenworth, Kans., 2006), pp. 101–23; p. 120.

23 M. M. Matthews, *The U.S. Army on the Mexican Border: A Historical Perspective* (Fort Leavenworth, Kans., 2007), p. 83.

5 A MULTITUDE OF CONFLICTS

1 A. Giustozzi, *Koran, Kalashnikov and Laptop: The Neo-Taliban Insurgency in Afghanistan* (London, 2007).

2 N. Aylwin-Foster, 'Changing the Army for Counterinsurgency Operations', *Military Review* (2005).

3 J. Fergusson, *A Million Bullets: The Real Story of the British Army in Afghanistan* (London, 2008).

4 S. Said, *Legitimizing Military Rule: Indonesian Armed Forces Ideology, 1958–2000* (Jakarta, 2006).

5 A. Levy and C. Scott-Clark, *Deception: Pakistan, the United States and the Global Nuclear Weapons Conspiracy* (New York, 2007); G. Perkovich, *India's Nuclear Bomb: The Impact on Global Proliferation* (Berkeley, Calif., 1999).

6 B. E. Bechtol, *Red Rogue: The Persistent Challenge of North Korea* (Dulles, Va., 2007); J. Becker, *Rogue Regime: Kim Jong II and the Looming Threat of North Korea* (Oxford, 2007); G.

D. Chang, *Nuclear Showdown: North Korea Takes on the World* (London, 2007); M. V. Creekmore, *A Moment of Crisis: Jimmy Carter, the Power of a Peacemaker, and North Korea's Nuclear Ambitions* (London, 2007).

6 INTO THE FUTURE I

1 R. Kagan, *The Return of History and the End of Dreams* (New York, 2008).

2 A. I. Johnston, *Cultural Realism: Strategic Culture and Grand Strategy in Chinese History* (Princeton, NJ, 1995).

3 T. Delpech, *Savage Century: Back to Barbarism* (Washington, DC, 2007), p. 133.

4 X. Li, *A History of the Modern Chinese Army* (Lexington, Ky., 2007).

5 BP data June 2008.

6 S. Chesterman and C. Lehnardt (eds), *From Mercenaries to Market: The Rise and Regulation of Private Military Companies* (Oxford, 2007).

7 B. M. Linn, *The Echo of Battle: The Army's Way of War* (Cambridge, Mass., 2007), pp. 240–1.

8 G. Adams and G. Ben-Ari, *Transforming European Militaries: Coalition Operations and the Technology Gap* (London, 2006).

9 J. Black, *The European Question and the National Interest* (London, 2006).

7 INTO THE FUTURE II

1 T. Homer-Dixon, *The Upside of Down: Catastrophe, Creativity and the Renewal of Civilization* (Washington, DC, 2007).

2 N. Mabey, *Delivering Climate Security: International Security Responses to a Climate Changed World* (London, 2008), pp. 80–1.

3 C. Kinsey, *Corporate Soldiers and International Security: The Rise of Private Military Companies* (Abingdon, 2006), p. 121.

4 S. Armstrong, *War PLC: The Rise of the New Corporate Mercenary* (London, 2008), p. 250.

5 R. Smith, *The Utility of Force: The Art of War in the Modern World* (London, 2005).

6 J.-L. Dufour and M. Vaisse, *La Guerre au XX siècle* (2nd edn, Paris, 2003), p. 217.

7 P. Bobbitt, *Terror and Consent: The Wars for the Twenty-First Century* (London, 2008).

8 CONCLUSIONS

1 R. Peters, 'The Future. Our Soldiers. Their Cities', *Parameters* (1996).

2 V. D. Hanson, 'Why Study War?' *Army History,* 68 (2008), pp. 26–32.

3 For a critique of Kennedy, see J. Black, *Great Powers and the Quest for Hegemony: The World Order Since 1500* (London, 2008).

4 M. Knox and W. Murray (eds), *The Dynamics of Military Revolution, 1300–2050* (Cambridge, 2001).

SELECTED FURTHER READING

Allard, K.. *Somalia Operations: Lessons Learned* (Washington, DC, 1995).

Bacevich, A. J. and Imbar, E. (eds), *The Gulf War of 1991 Reconsidered* (London, 2003).

Barnett, T., *The Pentagon's New Map: War and Peace in the Twenty-First Century* (London, 2004).

Beckett, I. F. W., *Modern Insurgencies and Counter-Insurgencies: Guerrillas and Their Opponents since 1750* (London, 2001).

Black, J., *The Dotted Red Line: Britain's Defence Policy in the Modern World* (London, 2006).

Bobbitt, P., *Terror and Consent: The Wars for the Twenty-First Century* (London, 2008).

Bowden, M., *Black Hawk Down: A Story of Modern War* (New York, 1999).

Clark, W., *Waging Modern War: Bosnia, Kosovo, and the Future of Combat* (New York, 2002).

Cordesman, A. H., *The Lessons of Afghanistan* (Washington, DC, 2002).

Cordesman, A. H. and Wagner, A. R., *The Lessons of Modern War, Vol. IV: The Gulf War* (Boulder, Col., 1996).

Creveld, M. V., *The Changing Face of War: Lessons of Combat, from the Marne to Iraq* (London, 2007).

Echevarria, A., *Fourth-Generation Warfare and Other Myths* (Carlisle, Pa., 2005).

Ferguson, B. (ed.), *The State, Identity, and Violence: Political Disintegration in the Post-Cold War World* (London, 2003).

Freedman, L., *The Revolution in Strategic Affairs* (Oxford, 1998).

Gray, C., *Another Bloody Century: Future Warfare* (London, 2005).

Jane's World Navies (London, 2008–).

Johnson, R., *A Region in Turmoil: South Asian Conflicts since 1947* (London, 2005).

—— *Oil, Islam and Conflict: Central Asia since 1945* (London, 2007).

Kaldor, M., *New and Old Wars: Organised Violence in a Global Era* (Stanford, Calif., 1999).

Lehman, J. F. and Sicherman, H. (eds), *America the Vulnerable: Our Military Problems and How To Fix Them* (Philadelphia, Pa., 2002).

Leonhard, R. R., *The Art of Maneuver: Maneuver-Warfare Theory and AirLand Battle* (Novato, Calif., 1991).

Linn, B. M. *The Echo of Battle: The Army's Way of War* (Cambridge, Mass., 2007).

Lonsdale, D., *The Nature of War in the Information Age* (London, 2004).

McNamee, T. (ed.), *War Without Consequences: Iraq's Insurgency and the Spectre of Strategic Defeat* (London, 2008).

Mandel, R., *The Meaning of Military Victory* (Boulder, Col., 2006).

Munkler, H., *The New Wars* (London, 2004).

Olsen, J. A., *Strategic Air Power in Desert Storm* (London, 2003).

Ovendale, R., *The Origins of the Arab-Israeli Wars* (4th edn, London, 2004).

Record, J., *Beating Goliath: Why Insurgencies Win* (Dulles, Va., 2007).

Reeve, S., *The New Jackals: Ramzi Yousef, Osama bin Laden and the Future of Terrorism* (Boston, Mass., 1999).

Ricks, T. E., *Fiasco: The American Military Adventure in Iraq* (London, 2006).

Scales, R. H., *Certain Victory: The US Army in the Gulf War* (Fort Leavenworth, Kans., 1993).

Shacochis, B., *The Immaculate Invasion* (New York, 1999).

Shapiro, I., *Containment: Rebuilding a Strategy against Global Terror* (Princeton, NJ, 2007).

Smith, R., *The Utility of Force: The Art of War in the Modern World* (London, 2005).

Swain, R. W., *'Lucky War': Third Army in Desert Storm* (Fort Leavenworth, Kans., 1994).

Till, G., *Seapower: A Guide for the Twenty-First Century* (London, 2004).

Utley, R., *The Case for Coalition-Motivation and Prospects: French Military Intervention in the 1990s* (Camberley, 2001).

Woodward, B., *Plan of Attack* (New York, 2004).

WALT DISNEY's

The Jungle Book

C000029689

PENGUIN BOOKS

Penguin Books Ltd, Harmondsworth,
Middlesex, England
Penguin Books, 625 Madison Avenue,
New York, New York 10022, U.S.A.
Penguin Books Australia Ltd, Ringwood,
Victoria, Australia
Penguin Books Canada Ltd, 2801 John Street,
Markham, Ontario, Canada L3R 1B4
Penguin Books (N.Z.) Ltd, 182-190 Wairau Road,
Auckland 10, New Zealand

First published in this format 1980

Copyright © 1980 Walt Disney Productions
All rights reserved

Made and printed in Great Britain by
The Fakenham Press Ltd, Norfolk

Except in the United States of America, this book is
sold subject to the condition that it shall not, by
way of trade or otherwise, be lent, re-sold, hired out,
or otherwise circulated without the publisher's prior
consent in any form of binding or cover other than
that in which it is published and without a similar
condition including this condition being imposed on
the subsequent purchaser

From the classical legend of Romulus and Remus to the comparatively recent fiction of Tarzan of the Apes, the idea of children reared by wolves and other beasts of the wild, has exercised a potent fascination. Not long after the appearance of Mowgli in 1894, a case of a wolf-boy was reported in the *Calcutta Statesman,* and subsequent scientific controversy has still not succeeded in distinguishing fact from mythology.

Rudyard Kipling almost certainly would have heard stories of feral children while he worked as a newspaperman in India. He had earned quite a reputation as a short-story writer, but it was not until he had left India that he was to invent the jungle world of Mowgli, Bagheera the Panther, Kaa the Python, Baloo the Bear and the villainous Shere Khan the Tiger.

While on a honeymoon world tour with his American wife, Caroline, Kipling received news that all his savings had been lost, with the collapse of an Orient banking company. Cashing in the unused portions of their travel tickets, the couple made for Brattleboro, Vermont, where Caroline's family lived, and it was here during a blizzard in a ten-dollar-a-week workman's cottage that *The Jungle Books* were born.

For many years Walt Disney tried to acquire the film rights. He thought that the stories were ideally suited to the cartoon medium, since Kipling had created such a marvellous cast of animal characters, with the kind of human traits that were almost custom-made for animation.

In 1963, the deal was clinched, and a three-and-a-half-year multi-million-dollar project was ready to get under way.

However, work could not begin immediately. *Winnie the Pooh* was in the studio, and there were inevitable difficulties in constructing a precise plot-line from a collection of stories. Walt Disney's advice to his scriptwriter, Larry Clemmons, was unequivocal. 'Here is the original by Rudyard Kipling. The first thing I want you to do is not to read it!'

Sadly, this was the last animated picture to be personally supervised by Disney. In the autumn of 1966 he was discovered to have cancer of the lung. He had an operation, but died six weeks later, at the age of sixty-five.

The Jungle Book was not quite finished, but Disney's influence on every aspect of the film was all-pervasive. 'I think a little of Walt rubbed off on all of us,' said the director Wolfgang Reitherman. 'He really had a vision. And he never lost the memory of what enthused him at the beginning . . .

'It was great to work under those conditions. We created characters from thin air. We made life happen in cartoon form. There were no movie actors to fall back on . . . From our imagination we created frame to frame spontaneity.

'We've sustained that feeling through our many cartoon features from *Snow White* to *The Jungle Book*, because no picture was ever made the same. We were always trying new techniques . . .

'In *The Jungle Book* we tried to incorporate the personalities of the actors that do the voices into the cartoon characters, and we came up with something totally different. When Phil Harris did the voice of Baloo, the carefree jungle bear, he gave it a bubble of life. We didn't coach him, just let it happen.

'All the rest of the characters evolved the same way. And as they grew in dimension, the story was altered . . . We always leave the plot loose enough so that the personalities meshing together enhance it by the natural action.'

The musical numbers also carried major strong points. 'We had to get right into the action,' said songwriter Dick Sherman, 'or the songs would slow the tempo of the picture, or get lost in the shuffle.' The result is a film that, perhaps, more than any other Disney feature has an extraordinarily infectious sense of fun and freewheeling spontaneity.

The novelist Rosemary Sutcliff wrote of the Kipling stories, 'The boy who has never run with Mowgli's wolf pack has missed something he will never get from any other writer.' Any child of any age who has not seen Disney's version has missed a very different kind of enchantment.

P. Sidey

Many strange legends are told of these jungles in India,
but none so strange as the story of a small boy named Mowgli.

It all began when the panther Bagheera heard an unfamiliar cry
that broke the silence of the jungle.

t occurred to Bagheera that a family of wolves
had been blessed with a litter of cubs.

The mother and cubs quickly took to the newcomer,

Akela: 'Shere Khan will kill the boy and all who protect him. He must leave the pack.'
Rama: 'But he's like my own son.'
Bagheera: 'I know of a man-village where he'll be safe.
I'll take him there.'

Bagheera and Mowgli set off for the village.
Mowgli: 'It's getting dark. When are we going home?'
Bagheera: 'This time we're not returning. Shere Khan hates two things
– fire and man. He has come back to the jungle and has sworn to kill you.'
Mowgli: 'Well, I'm not afraid. I can look after myself.'

By the ranks or single file
Over every jungle mile
We stamp and crush through the underbush
In a military style.'

Mowgli: 'Hello, what are you doing? Can I do it too?'
Baby: 'Of course. Do what I do, but don't talk in ranks.
It's against regulations.'

Colonel Hathi: 'Inspection! Arms!'

Colonel Hathi: 'A dusty muzzle! Soldiers, remember that in battle a trunk can save your life.'

Colonel Hathi: 'Ha ha – a new recruit.
I say, what happened to your trunk?'

Colonel Hathi: 'A mancub! This is treason. I'll have no mancub in my jungle.'
Mowgli: 'It's not *your* jungle.'
Bagheera: 'Now now, Mowgli. I can explain, Colonel. I'm taking him back
to the man-village to stay. You have the word of Bagheera.'

Colonel Hathi: 'Let's get on with it. Right foot . . .

. . . and forward march!'
Bagheera: 'Let's get out of here before anything else happens.'

Bagheera: 'That does it. I've had it. From now on you're on your own!'

Mowgli wanders off,

but soon feels lonely.

Baloo: Well now, what have we here? What a pretty thing this is!'
Mowgli: 'Go away!'
Baloo: That's big talk for a little one.'
Mowgli: 'I'm big enough.'

Baloo: 'You need help and old Baloo's going to teach you to fight like a bear.'

Baloo: 'Now give me a big bear growl like this. Scare me!'

Bagheera: 'What a terrifying growl! Mowgli must be in trouble.'

Baloo: 'I . . . can't stand . . . ha . . . that tickling.
We don't do that here in the jungle. Anyway, what are you doing here?'
Mowgli: 'Bagheera was taking me to the man-village.'

Mowgli: 'Oh Baloo, I want to stay with you.'
Baloo: 'You'll be safe with me. All you need are
  The "bare" necessities,
  The simple "bare" necessities of life.'

Baloo and Mowgli: 'Look for the bare necessities
The simple bare necessities,

Forget about your worries and your strife,
That's why a bear can rest at ease
With just the bare necessities of life.'

Baloo: 'Come on, Bagheera, join in the song.'

Mowgli: 'Oh Baloo, this is perfect.'

Bagheera: 'I give up. Well, I hope their luck holds out.'

Baloo: 'Mowgli, how about flicking that fly off your papa bear's nose.'

Baloo: 'Stop! Take your flea-picking hands off my cub!'

Bagheera: All right, what happened? Where is Mowgli?'
Baloo: 'Thousands of those mangy monkeys
ambushed us and carried him off to the ancient ruins.'

Mowgli: 'Baloo! Help me! They're carrying me away.'

Bagheera: 'The ancient ruins! Oh I hate to think what will happen when he meets Louie, King of the Apes.'

Monkeys: 'We caught him, King Louie. Here he is.'
King Louie: 'So you're the mancub.'

King Louie: 'I want to walk like you,
Talk like you,
You see it's true,
An ape like me
Can learn to be a human too.'

Bagheera: 'Now, Baloo, while you create a disturbance, I'll rescue Mowgli.'

Baloo dresses up as an ape and dances wildly with King Louie.

While everyone is dancing, Bagheera lies in wait on the crumbling ruins.

Suddenly King Louie sees through Baloo's disguise.

Bagheera makes a vain attempt to snatch Mowgli,

but Baloo is more successful,

leaving King Louie surrounded by the ruins of his temple.

Mowgli sleeps soundly after their escape from the ruined temple,
while Bagheera and Baloo discuss his future.

Bagheera: 'Mowgli obviously can't look after himself in the jungle,
      the sooner you get him to the man-village the better.'

The next morning Baloo and Mowgli leave Bagheera and wander off into the jungle.

Mowgli: 'I do like being a bear. I'll live here in the jungle all my life.'

Baloo: 'But, Mowgli, I must take you to the man-village.
With Shere Khan around it's not safe for you here.'
Mowgli: 'But you said we were friends. You're as bad as Bagheera . . .'

Mowgli rushes off into the jungle, leaving a lonely Baloo.

While out hunting, Shere Khan hears Colonel Hathi drilling his troops.

Bagheera: 'Halt! I need your help . . . it's an emergency . . . we've lost the mancub!'
Colonel Hathi: 'Well, it serves him right.'

Shere Khan: 'A lost mancub! How delightful!'

Mother Elephant: 'Hathi, this has gone far enough.
How would you like to have *our* boy lost and alone in the jungle?'
Colonel Hathi: 'That's a different matter. Well, all right,
I'll send out a patrol.'

Colonel Hathi: 'Volunteers for a special mission will step one pace forward.'
Shere Khan (listening): 'Element of surprise – ha!
Now for my rendezvous with the little lost mancub.'

Mowgli has spent the day wandering through the jungle,

and settles down on a narrow 'branch'.

Kaa: 'Oh mancub, s-s-so nice to s-s-see you again.
Now let me look at you.
Mowgli: 'No, this time I know what you're trying to do.'

Kaa: 'Is there anything I can do to help you?'
Mowgli: 'You mean . . . how could you do that?'
Kaa: 'I can see to it that you never have to leave this jungle.
But you must trust me.'

Kaa (singing): 'Trus-s-st in me . . .
Jus-s-st in me;
You can sleep s-s-safe and s-s-sound,
Knowing I am around.'

feeling very much alone.

Vultures: Just look at him! He must be down on his luck.'
Mowgli: 'No one wants me around.'

Vultures: 'We'll be your friends.
We'd like to make you an honorary vulture.'

Shere Khan creeps up and Mowgli's new friends
instantly abandon him, leaving him to face the tiger alone.

Shere Khan: 'You're trying my patience.'

At the crucial moment Baloo appears, but gets badly attacked.

At last the vultures come to Mowgli's help. While one strikes
at Shere Khan's eyes, the others lift Mowgli out of danger.

and the terrified tiger runs off into the jungle.

Mowgli then sees the brave Baloo lying silently on the battle scene.

But Baloo regains consciousness and listens with delight as his friends talk lovingly of him.

Mowgli: 'Baloo! You're alive! You certainly had us worried.'
Baloo: 'Nothing is ever going to come between us again.'

Baloo: 'Oh Bagheera, it's too bad you missed the action.
You should have seen me, making fun of that old tiger.

Mowgli: 'Look, what's that?'
Bagheera: Oh, it's the man-village.'

The girl waits shyly for Mowgli

but pretends not to notice him as she returns
to the village.

On the way she deliberately drops the pot . . .

so he can refill it,

and follow her back to the village.

After a moment of indecision he decides to remain in the village with his new friend.

Bagheera: 'It was bound to happen. Mowgli is now where he belongs.'
Baloo: 'I still think he'd have made a wonderful bear.

Well, come on, let's get back to where *we* belong!'

MY FIRS CALCULATOR

LEARN TO COUNT WITH THE TEDDY BEARS

WRITTEN BY MARION ELLIOT

ILLUSTRATED BY
JENNY TULIP

This is the teddy bear's calculator.
What do all the buttons do?

Number display

Dividing button

Multiplying button

Subtracting button

Adding button

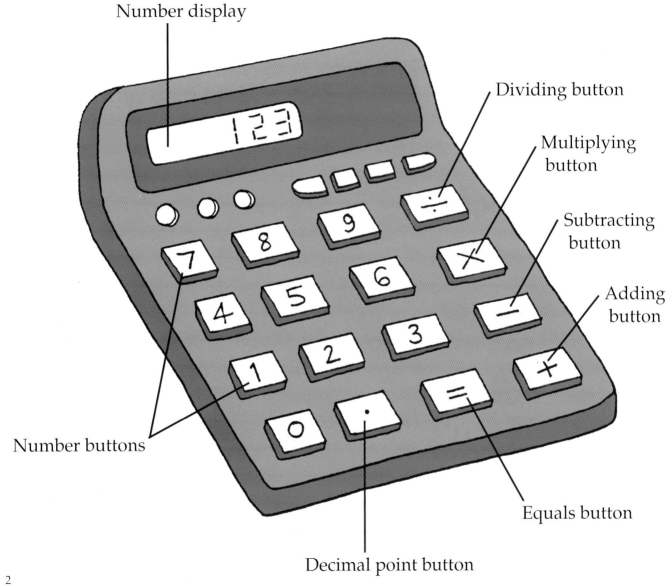

Number buttons

Equals button

Decimal point button

Each teddy bear has a number on its t-shirt.
Can you find the same number on your calculator?
Use two numbers to make 10.

Learn about adding

Can you help teddy bear to do these sums on your calculator?

Adding

+ This is the adding button. It is used for adding numbers together and counting thir

4 + 7 = 11

Can you add up these cars?

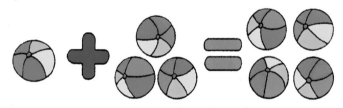

1 + 2 = 3

How many rubber balls?

1 + 3 = 4

Now see if you can add together these bananas.

1 + 4 = 5

How many blue things can you add up?
And how many red? How many things are blue and red?

1 flowery hat

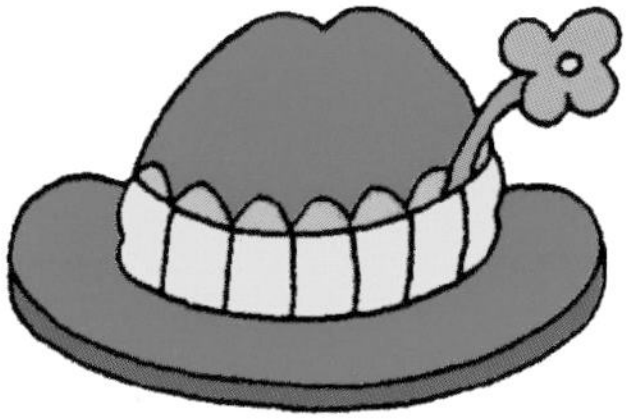

1 telephone

1 smelly sock

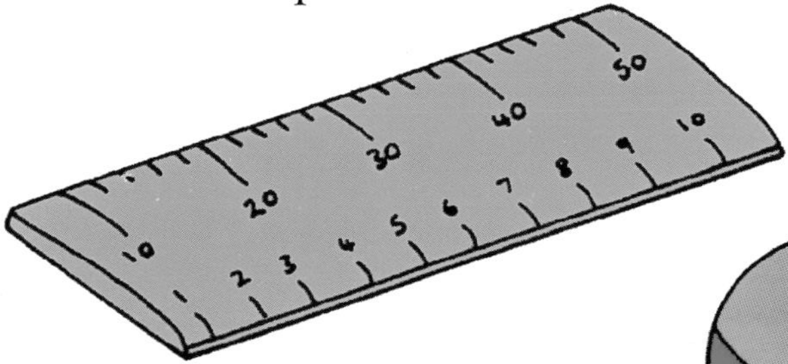

1 straight ruler

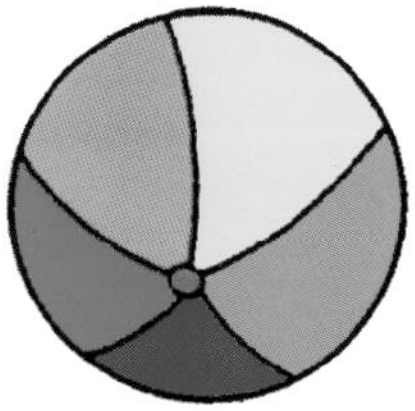

1 bouncy ball

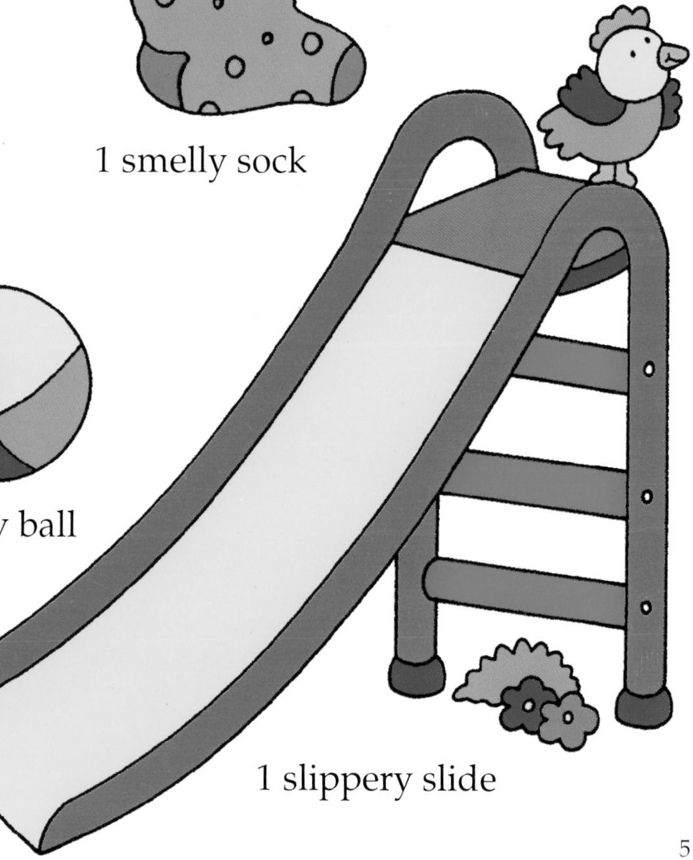

1 cowboy hat

1 slippery slide

Teddy bear is adding up all the animals.
How many can you see?

Learn about subtracting

Can you help teddy bear do these subtraction sums? Use the ⊟ button on your calculator.

Subtracting

⊟ This is the subtracting button. It is used for taking one number away from another.

10 - 8 = 2

2 kittens - 1 kitten = 1 kitten

5 dinosaurs - 1 dinosaur = 4 dinosaurs

8

Can you count all the flowers in the top picture?
And the bottom one? If you take the smaller from
the larger, how many flowers are left?

Answer
4
(13 - 9 =4)

Learn about multiplying

Can you help teddy bear
using your ⌧ button?

Multiplying

⌧ This is the
multiplying
or times button.
It is used to make
one number
bigger by using
another number.

5 x 3 = 15

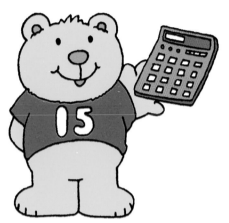

How many does 2 times 3 fish make?

See if you can do these sums
using the ⏹️ button on your calculator.

2 x 2 = 4

3 x 4 = 12

11

Learn about dividing

How many times will a small number go into a large one?

2 bananas will fit into 6 bananas 3 times

$6 \div 2 = 3$

Dividing
⊡ This is the dividing button. It is used to work out how many times one number will fit into another.

$12 \div 4 = 3$

See if you can do these sums with teddy bear using your ÷ button.

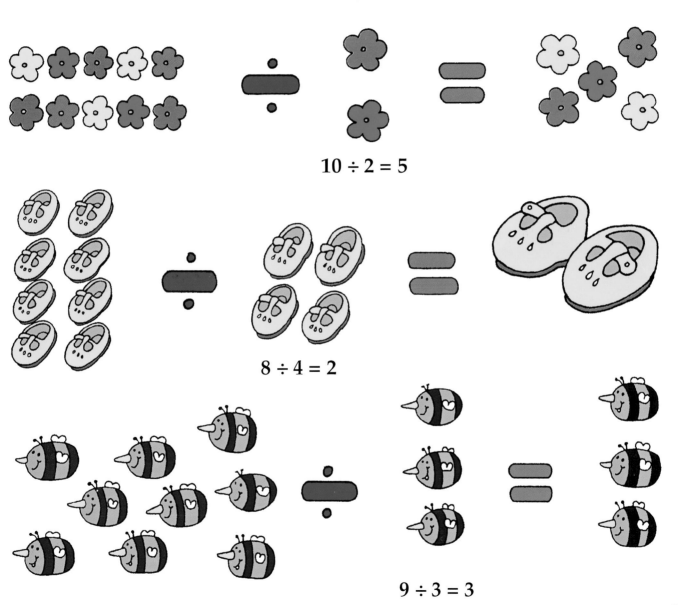

$10 \div 2 = 5$

$8 \div 4 = 2$

$9 \div 3 = 3$

13

Help teddy bear to do this big sum using your ⊞, ⊟, ⊠ and ⊡ keys. Good luck!

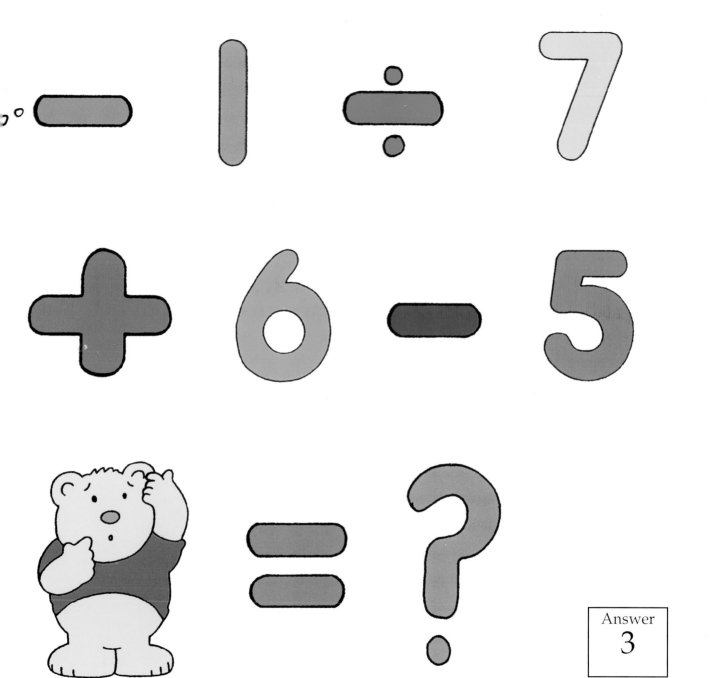

Answer
3

15

Adding large numbers

The teddy bears are adding these big numbers
together using their ➕ button.
Can you help them?

60 + 90 = 150
1000 + 60 = 1060
1000 + 90 = 1090

Multiplying large numbers

Now help them to multiply these big numbers using the ☒ button.
How many different sums can you make?

$100 \times 70 = 7000$
$20 \times 50 = 1000$
$100 \times 20 = 2000$

The teddy bears have worked hard and now they want to play.
Can you add all the numbers in the building bricks?
And the balloons and juggling balls?

See how much fun the teddy bears are having with these numbers!

Now it is night-time. Teddy bear is still counting in his sleep!

© 1996 Anness Publishing Ltd, 88-89 Blackfriars Road, London SE1 8HA